Primero Dios

Hispanic Liturgical Resource

Acknowledgments

Liturgy Training Publications agradece profundamente a Koch Foundation, Inc. por la generosa contribución y apoyo manifestado a fin de llevar a cabo la publicación de este libro, *Primero Dios*.

El propósito de este libro es evangelizar y propagar las múltiples expresiones de la fe católica del Pueblo Hispano que radica en los Estados Unidos de Norteamérica.

Primero Dios was edited by Martin F. Connell; Deborah Bogaert was the production editor, with assistance from Theresa Houston and Miguel Arias. The art for the book is by Guillermo Delgado. The book was designed by Barb Rohm. The production artist, Mark Hollopeter, set the book in Minion and Matrix. Printed in the United States of America.

10 09 08 07 06   7 6 5 4 3

Library of Congress Catalog Card number 97-71349

ISBN-10: 1-58654-142-2
ISBN-13: 978-1-58654-142-6
CUSTOM

Primero Dios

Hispanic Liturgical Resource

Mark R. Francis, CSV
Arturo Pérez-Rodríguez

LITURGY
TRAINING
PUBLICATIONS

Contents

115

A Note from the Authors

T hose engaged in Hispanic ministry in the United States are constantly called upon — especially if they have been trained in seminaries and theology schools in this country — to bridge two conceptual and imaginative worldviews. The first worldview is that of twentieth-century North American Catholicism. This vision of church and gospel is conditioned by the ordered, logical and individualistic aspects of U.S. culture that emphasize creativity and personal achievement. The second worldview, that of the growing number of Hispanic/Latino Catholics, is characterized by a much more affective notion of reality: Life only really finds meaning in relationship with others. Hispanics find identity and meaning first and foremost in belonging to a particular family, in having a particular set of *compadres*, in being a member of *la raza*. Given the difference between these two worlds, it is not surprising that religious celebrations, which express and celebrate the relationships between ourselves, God and one another, are approached from different angles by these two cultures. For Hispanics, practices of popular religion are closely allied with relationships and thus constitute the traditional way by which the rites of the church have been adapted and modified to express their world of relationships, their world of meaning.

This book is the fruit of a dialogue between mainstream U.S. Catholic culture and Hispanic/Latino culture as it is lived in the United States. It arises from the conviction that effective liturgical ministry within the Hispanic community must take into account the traditional way in which Hispanics have approached liturgy and prayer — through the practices of popular religion. We embrace the refinement and definition of popular religion as stated in the *Puebla* document of the Latin American Bishops, 444:

> By the religion of the people, popular religiosity, or popular piety (*Evangelii Nuntiandi*, 48), we mean the whole complex of underlying beliefs rooted in God, the basic attitudes that flow from these beliefs, and the expressions that manifest them. It is the form of cultural life that religion takes on among a given people. In its most characteristic cultural form, the religion of the Latin American people is an expression of the Catholic faith. It is a people's Catholicism. (as translated in *Puebla and Beyond,* John Eagleson and Philip Scharper, eds., New York: Orbis, 1979, 184.)

Gratefully, studies continue to be done on popular religion in general and on popular Catholicism in particular. For the purposes of this resource book, we understand popular Catholicism to be the interpretation and enrichment of the official rites of the Catholic church by the Hispanic community. Ministers, both Hispanic and non-Hispanic, respond pastorally to the need to bridge the popular with the official by validating the religious experience of the *pueblo* and at the same time celebrating the blessings that the liturgical renewal of Vatican II has brought to the whole church.

We offer this resource to all who minister liturgically within the Hispanic community: priests, deacons, seminarians and lay ministers in training. More than simply a source of information on integrating popular religious practices within the liturgy, these pages promote an attitude of dialogue between and respect for the "official liturgy" and the rites of the people. We are convinced that it is this dialogue that makes it possible for us to be more present to one another and to God.

The expertise in liturgy and language of Rosa Maria Icaza, CCVI, contributed significantly to this work; we thank her for her helpful comments. We also are grateful for the valuable dialogue with Tim Matovina, Roberto Goizueta and Miguel Arias, and the helpful recommendations they offered in reading this material. Guillermo Delgado's artwork enhances, expresses and invites us into the beauty of what we write. Martin Connell, our editor, has been a faithful companion on the path to transforming an idea into a reality.

In reality, there is no conclusion to this resource book. The dialogue of inculturation calls us to go beyond understanding the liturgical expression of our faith as merely a set of propositions about God. This dialogue encourages us to approach God with our whole being, emotions as well as intellect, body as well as spirit. This dialogue never really ends.

Hispanic Popular Religion and Liturgy

Why a Hispanic Liturgical Resource?

hy a liturgical resource for Hispanic ministry in the United States? Because for many pastoral ministers working with the growing number of Hispanics/Latinos in the United States — especially those ministers who have not had the opportunity to live "full time" in a Latino culture — the "traditional" popular religious customs of Hispanics/Latinos are often misunderstood, as is their relationship to the "official" liturgical celebrations of the church presented in the liturgical books. Priests, liturgists, catechists and other pastoral agents trained in the United States are sometimes bewildered and frustrated by Hispanic popular religion, especially when it "intrudes upon" the celebration of key sacramental rites and threatens to violate what many have learned as "good liturgical practice." This book was designed to bridge what is often perceived as the gulf between the religious experience of the people and the liturgical principles of the official books. This gulf can be illustrated by the following conversations, which are often heard in Hispanic parishes.

"Father, we can't have the baby baptized right away because the *padrinos* we have chosen live out of town. But can we do a *Presentación del niño* (presentation of the child at the church) next Sunday?" — *We don't do that kind of thing here, and anyway, it's not one of the rites of the church.*

"Our daughter is going to turn fifteen next year. How can we arrange for a *Quinceañera?*" — *We don't do that kind of thing at this parish. It's a needless expense for the parents and relatives, and besides, it's not one of the rites of the church.*

"*Padrecito,* when do you place the large *lazo* around the necks of the newlyweds during the nuptial Mass?" — *I've never heard of that custom. Anyway, we don't do that kind of thing here, and besides, it's not one of the rites of the church.*

We don't do that kind of thing here. It's not one of the rites of the church. It is not uncommon for Hispanics to be turned away with a general dismissal of their religious customs. Sometimes their requests are met with an even more specific critique of their traditions as, at best, meaningless ritualism, or at worst, just plain superstition. However, the negative reaction of U.S. pastoral ministers to popular religious practices does not usually stem from a lack of compassion or an honest desire to minister effectively to the Hispanic community. Many well-meaning parish ministers regard these customs as irreconcilably at odds with good liturgical and pastoral practice because of the training they have received in seminaries or theological schools — a training that unconsciously defined the "standard," or normative, interpretation of the church's liturgy from the perspective of white, middle-class North America. Even those who have taken the trouble to learn Spanish may not be familiar with these elements of popular religion and are at a loss to integrate them into the pastoral strategy of the parish. This integration seems less than urgent when ministers ask the people to explain their customs and to give reasons for why they want them included in the official celebrations of the sacraments. Often the people who are asked cannot give a detailed explanation describing the origin and "meaning" as these rites — other than the fact that they are traditions. Frustrated by the lack of clarity, desiring to be authentic and sincere in their role of presiders at prayer, and unable to reconcile these rites with liturgical norms, presiders ignore the requests and strive, through education, to move the people beyond the need for popular religion into the practices of the "mainstream" church.

It is undeniable that there are elements of superstition in some of the practices of Hispanic popular religion. Therefore, many pastoral agents tell themselves that the principal challenge in Hispanic ministry is developing a suitable catechesis to help people get beyond their attachment to statues and novenas. Besides, isn't this move from a naive and sometimes superstitious devotionalism to a more "mature" Christianity the experience of most Euro-American groups after Vatican II?

This approach and the attitude that supports it need to be challenged. This approach uncritically assumes that the role of a minister is to make the lives of the people with whom one ministers more like one's own life. It does not take into account that the spirit that animates the *liturgical* life of many of the Hispanic peoples here in the United States is strongly influenced by the traditions of what is termed "popular religion." Born of the often traumatic union of the religious worldviews of the Spanish, Native American and African peoples, these customs are often ritual expressions of a people's identity and dignity, forged in the crucible of oppression and unspeakable hardship. They have grown up alongside the official rites of the church and serve as the context in which the sacraments are often celebrated. Many popular religious practices originated during the period of the first evangelization of the New World. They often began as customs that gave meaning to religious concepts that were difficult for the native peoples to understand because they were at odds with their culture. Hispanic "popular religion" is more correctly understood as an inculturation of the gospel. It is the product of a living dialogue between the culture of the people and the word of God. While never definitive or complete, this dialogue is dynamic and continues today in parishes throughout the United States. In order to appreciate the place that popular religion occupies in the religious imagination of Hispanics, an acquaintance with an outline of the history of its genesis and its relationship to the official liturgy of the church and to European devotionalism may be useful.

Notes from History: Liturgy and European Devotionalism

For centuries before the Second Vatican Council, the official worship of the Roman Catholic church was largely defined by the duly approved liturgical books. Concerned with curbing medieval abuses and with countering the challenge to the traditional liturgy raised by Protestant reformers in the sixteenth century, the Council of Trent mandated that the pope issue official versions of liturgical celebrations through the newly centralized Congregation of Rites, seated in Rome. These books were to reflect the faith of the church by presenting not only the prayer texts themselves but also detailed ceremonial directions describing how the celebration of the Mass and other sacraments was to be carried out. This goal of a purified liturgy was greatly aided by the invention of the printing press in the previous century. Because of this new technology, it was possible for the first time in history to standardize the worship life of the Western church by issuing ritual books that did not vary from one another — as had the previous, handwritten books. The unchanging and uniform celebration of the Mass became a hallmark of Catholicism after the Council of Trent (1545–1563). It was often said that one could go anywhere in the world and the Mass would be celebrated the same way.

However, this was never completely the case, for books do not "do" liturgy — people do liturgy. Pages don't celebrate, people do. For example, the celebration of the Mass in a rococo cathedral in Austria to the strains of a Mass composed by Mozart and sung by a large choir with full orchestra was obviously a different experience than a furtive low Mass celebrated without music (and illegally) in Ireland during the period of the penal laws of the eighteenth century. The prayer texts and the priest's actions were basically the same in both cases, but the *context* made even this uniform rite a very different experience. Even the Tridentine liturgical books left a great deal of leeway to local custom in the celebration of sacraments other than the eucharist. For this reason, even before Vatican II the celebration of many sacraments — marriage is a good example — varied greatly from place to place.

Generally, though, the Tridentine reform of the liturgy encouraged a legalistic uniformity in liturgical rites. In Europe, the effects of this reform were felt on various levels. In purifying the Mass liturgy, the Missal of Pius V (1570) tended to turn the celebration of the Mass, and by extension the other sacraments, into an activity monopolized by clergy. The people "heard" Mass or simply "received" the sacraments, but no one considered lay people as "doing" the liturgy in an active sense. From the Council of Trent to Vatican II, the Roman Rite was characterized by an emphasis on orthodox expression of the faith through a strict adherence to the rubrics or ceremonial directives, at the expense of a more poetic or emotive approach to worship. The language of the rite, Latin, also served to distance the average worshiper from the emotional content of even the more lyrical prayers of the Mass. The official liturgy of the church, however, never exhausted the impetus among the Christian people to pray. Novenas and other devotional rites allowed people to publicly express a most important dimension to religious experience: emotion. Since the official rites were dominated by the clergy and gave no place to spontaneous feelings, European devotionalism tended to make up for this lack by featuring feelings of joy and sorrow—sometimes to the point of exaggeration.

Although not exclusively controlled by the hierarchy, European devotionalism was largely encouraged by bishops and priests as a means of complementing the rites of the church and of shoring up national identity, especially when these devotions were brought from Europe to North America. Emphasis on the affective side of human life is also a hallmark of the popular religion that developed in the Spanish and Portuguese territories of the New World. The passionate nature of the Catholicism of the Iberian peninsula was also marked by centuries of struggle with the Moslems of Spain, which ended in 1492 with the expulsion of the Moors and Jews by "the most Catholic" sovereigns Isabela and Fernando. The militant medieval Catholicism brought by the Spaniards and Portuguese, wedded with the lively tradition of popular expressions of the faith practiced in these countries, serves then as one of the foundations for what we know today as Hispanic popular religion.

Hispanic Popular Religion

In addition to its connection to European devotionalism, Hispanic popular religion owes its origin to the confluence of religious sensitivities of two other cultural traditions: the Native American and the African.

Though far from uniform, Hispanic popular religion can be distinguished from its European counterpart by the fact it was neither dominated nor exclusively promoted by the clergy. On a continent that for a long time lacked the numbers of priests enjoyed by Europe and North America, Hispanic popular religion served to root Christianity in the lives of the new Christians in ways that the official liturgy could not.

Religion and religious customs were largely handed on from one generation to another by the women of the household. It is the women who pray and function in many ways as the "domestic priests" of Hispanic culture. It is they who intercede for the family in their prayers at the home *altarcito;* it is they who often lead the family in prayer. Though seeking the sacraments as a natural expression of faith, many Hispanics would not make the hard and fast distinction between the church's "liturgy" and "popular devotions" — for to them, both are prayer. We must remember, though, that it was popular religious practice that sustained the Christian faith of generations in Latin America — in large part without the direct involvement of the officially sanctioned ministers of the church.

Popular religious customs often developed from catechetical strategies devised by missionaries to explain the faith to the native peoples. The catechetical origin of *Las Posadas,* for example, lies in the Augustinian friars' attempt to produce a kind of sacred play that would dramatize the story of Mary and Joseph's search for lodging prior to the birth of Jesus. Other practices of popular religion directly celebrate the sacredness of the home. Long called *religión casera,* or domestic religion, popular religious practices were largely taught and presided over by the women of the household. It is this characteristic that helps give Hispanic Catholicism its distinctive identity. Other practices stem from the influence of Native American customs and those brought by the Spaniards. For example, the popularity of Ash Wednesday among most Hispanics attests to an almost visceral link with the land and nature. It also continues the practice of the ritual manipulation of ashes practiced in many of the Native American religions. Finally, the influence of African religious sensibilities, more strongly felt in the Caribbean and in Brazil, emphasizes a sacred cosmos in which people live and move.

Most importantly, however, the ritual elements of popular religion that have made their way into the official liturgical celebration of the church serve to illustrate and celebrate relationships — especially those relationships that flow from the celebration of the stages of life that are lived in God's presence. The people's relationship with a loving Creator, and parents' relationship with children and *padrinos,* who are part of the extended family, are privileged places where God reveals the divine plan. While not all aspects of popular religion are free of problems, popular religious practices critiqued in the light of the scriptures and the teachings of Vatican II are an extremely important reference for the continuing inculturation of the liturgy within a Hispanic *ambiente.*

For this reason, in one of the most important pastoral statements since Vatican II — the document produced by the Puebla Conference (1979) — Latin American bishops challenged the church at large to help "the liturgy and the common people's piety cross-fertilize each other, giving lucid and prudent direction to the impulses of prayer and charismatic vitality that are evident today" (3.4.e). In the United States, the National Pastoral Plan for Hispanic Ministry (1987) echoes the concern of *Puebla* for an appropriate integration of popular religious practices in evangelizing Hispanics, in understanding their spirituality and in celebrating the faith. After speaking about the importance of Mary and the saints in the *mística* (the cultural context of Hispanic spirituality), the bishops describe popular religion as the place where the spirituality is incarnated: "a home of living relationships, a family, a community." This spirituality, though, is not dogmatic or propositional. For this reason, it is not always possible for someone who is Hispanic to explain in rational propositions why a devotion or a particular devotional practice is so important to him or her. As the bishops point out, "[Hispanic spirituality] will find expression more in ordinary life than in theory." In other words, actions speak louder than words. The bishops also go on to say that they hope that the pastoral plan will be "an encouragement for enriching liturgical celebration with cultural expressions of faith. It seeks to free the Spirit who is alive in the gatherings of our people" (8). These comments of the bishops, of course, are particularly important for inculturating worship in a Hispanic context.

How to Use this Liturgical Resource

The rituals presented in this book are not meant to be prepackaged liturgies; nor are they replacements for the official ritual books. Rather, they are meant to serve as models for liturgical celebrations within the Hispanic community in the United States. The reader needs to be aware that due to lack of space, not all of the pastoral options for a given rite are presented here. For this reason, we urge ministers preparing the celebration of the sacraments to become familiar with the rich contents of the official books—the pastoral introductions as well as the ritual options. Therefore, while not a replacement for the official books, this resource seeks to provide rituals that appropriately incorporate the customary elements of popular religion common to many Hispanics.

Many of the rites presented in this resource take place during Mass, and for this reason it is assumed in the text that a priest will preside. This is not meant to leave the impression that deacons and others in the community such as *rezanderos* (literally "those who pray") should not preside or assist the priest. Given the important role of the Hispanic permanent deacon in many parishes, it is he who will often be charged with these celebrations. Many of these rites do not have to take place during Mass and can easily be adapted to accommodate the circumstances of a presider who is not a priest. Lay people, such as *rezanderos*, are important pastoral leaders within the Hispanic community, and as such often assume a crucial role at celebrations such as *novenarios para un difunto* (the "novena," or prayer service, that takes place for nine consecutive nights after death).

None of these models is an attempt to present a "pure" cultural celebration, a representation of that which is done back in the "old country." This is because there are no "pure" celebrations in the United States; the cultural base in which most Hispanics move is changing every day. Not only do Hispanics in this country come from a wide range of backgrounds — Mexican, Caribbean, Central and South American — but they also are constantly influenced by the surrounding culture of North America, by its language as well as by its cultural norms. For this reason, it is impossible to present the Hispanic celebration of a given sacrament or popular rite. Since the people who are celebrating the sacraments are in the process of dynamic change and are in constant interaction with a variety of cultures, and since "people do liturgy," the rites themselves will have to take this reality into account. The pastoral ministers planning such celebrations need to be aware that they themselves must adapt the rites to their own situation and take the time to prepare them adequately.

Pastoral Method

A common understanding of inculturation describes it as the dynamic dialogue between our received religious traditions, both official and popular, and the particular culture in which they are celebrated. We would propose that the adaptation and inculturation of the rites follow a pastoral method that is respectful of the people's experience and encompasses four steps, or moments: 1) listening to the experience of the people; 2) entering into dialogue with the tradition; 3) developing a tentative new liturgy; 4) evaluating the rite in the light of the gospel in an ongoing fashion.

First, we need to start from the experience of the people. Not surprisingly, to discover this experience we need to ask the people about their customs and what they believe is happening in a given celebration, and pray with them in these celebrations as an active participant. It is only after this conversation that we can then turn to the official liturgical books and appreciate the richness contained in them for the Hispanic community. Thirdly, the result of this dialogue must be a blending, or "cross-fertilization," of the faith experience of the people with the larger traditions of the church mediated by the scriptures and the liturgical books. The fourth and last step of evaluation is the most difficult, yet the most crucial: Ultimately, our efforts at liturgical inculturation should be ordered to a more effective and eloquent proclamation of Jesus Christ risen from the dead. Inculturation in and of itself is not the goal; helping people to live their lives in greater fidelity to Christ and to see their lives reflected in the liturgical expressions of the church is the most important objective of this process.

Pastoral Context

In order to root these ritual models in pastoral experience, and in an effort to explain the relationships celebrated by the sacraments and by the elements of popular religion, we will attempt to present these celebrations in context, with reference to the flesh-and-blood human beings who celebrate them. For this reason, we have created representative pastoral situations, which include scenarios and people, that are often found in Hispanic parishes. Each chapter of the book—"Rites of Early Childhood,"

"Rites of Later Childhood," "Rites of Betrothal and Marriage," and finally, "Rites Associated with Sickness and Death," will discuss the impact these celebrations have on the lives of the family and on the pastoral style of the ministers of the parish. We hope that this narrative presentation, more than an abstract description alone, will help to describe the relationships that give life to all good liturgical celebrations and illustrate the old truism that people, not books, do the liturgy.

We are very much aware that this manner of presenting the rites reflects a developmental model for the sacraments. Using human maturation as an analogue to explain sacramental moments is being increasingly challenged by the *Order of Christian Initiation of Adults* and its manner of presenting adult initiation as the normative way of engaging in conversion to the gospel and entry into the church. Nevertheless, we decided that this presentation of the sacraments through the life cycle would be a more useful approach, since it reflects the predominant experience of these rites within the Hispanic/Latino community.

Now, meet the people who will help us appreciate the Hispanic *mística,* or context, for the celebration of the sacraments.

The Parents: Manuel and Carmen

Manuel and Carmen were married after a three-year on-again, off-again courtship. Manuel was not sure if he really wanted to continue his education, while Carmen was not sure she really wanted to settle down. Sixteen years ago, when both of them reached their twenty-fifth birthday, they came to realize that what they really wanted was to be together — so he proposed and she accepted. Their wedding united not only the two of them but also the differences in their respective family backgrounds. Manuel is Mexican American and Carmen is Puerto Rican.

Manuel's parents had crossed the border together when U.S. immigration policies were more tolerant. Manuel is first-generation

Latino. He had briefly considered priesthood when he was younger and had even entered the local seminary. It was there that he learned to appreciate the religious traditions of his family. These traditions created a spiritual hunger within him, and so he insisted on following the "old ways" when he got married, even though he was not always able to explain the meaning of these customs. He often argues with the parish priest about these matters.

Carmen's family had been living in this city for many generations. An extrovert, she felt at home crossing cultural barriers in reaching out to others in friendship. Having been raised in a family that prides itself on being *católico*, religious traditions are like "rice and beans" to her; they are part of her everyday world. Her confusion comes in defining what is "American" — or "Mexican" or "Puerto Rican" for that matter, since she was raised in a mixture of several cultural traditions.

Manuel and Carmen both wanted children immediately. Jesús was born eleven months after they were married. He was followed by Belén, a girl who is the spitting image of her mother. A few months ago, Natividad, their second girl, was born.

Los Padrinos: the Godparents, Jon and Ana

Jon has been Manuel's best friend since first grade, when Jon was a pudgy Polish youngster. The two met during a free-for-all fight on the playground. As they sat in the principal's outer office, they started talking to one another and immediately hit it off. From that day on their friendship grew, and they've never since stopped sharing personal, family and community stories.

So why did they wait until their third child to ask Jon to be a *padrino?* When Natividad was born, Manuel and Carmen asked him. Although not Hispanic, Jon knew the responsibilities that went with being a padrino. As Manuel's close friend, he always knew the day would come.

Ana is the sister of Carmen's first employer. Thier friendship, between a salvadoreña and a puertoriqueña, is unique. Their histories seem almost opposing and they did not become close friends until Ana began sharing how much she missed her homeland and her family — her "life's breath," as she put it. Coming to this new land and this new city was a threatening, heart-wrenching experience. As much as Carmen was at home here, Ana remained nostalgic for her native country, its people, climate and customs. Carmen grew to understand and appreciate Ana and asked her to be Natividad's *madrina* even before she approached Manuel with the idea.

The Clergy: Kevin, the priest, and Carlos, the permanent deacon

Father Kevin's ancestors had come to this country from Ireland and England several generations ago. To many people, this made him a native-born "American." It is said in his family that Kevin owes his feisty temperament to his Irish background. As a young boy, he settled many more arguments in the alleys with his fists than with reasoned debate. When he was assigned to St. Martín de Porres parish, a Hispanic bastion, he could barely speak Spanish. He took to studying Spanish the way he had formerly taken to the alleys, and soon he could defend himself eloquently and effectively. He soon found out, though, that learning a language was one thing, and understanding Hispanic ways and traditions of prayer was quite another. He reluctantly follows many of these customs out of respect for the people. He and Manuel are natural combatants who have grown through the years to agree to disagree.

Carlos, born in Mexico, is the parish's first permanent deacon — though when it comes to Manuel and Kevin, Carlos's role is more like that of a parish referee. Carlos has the rare privilege of knowing most of the parishioners, since he is the veteran member of the parish pastoral team. He has the wisdom of age and has developed his natural disposition to get along. His own decision to become a permanent deacon rested mainly on the fact that he knew how to bring out the best in people, which he has proved again and again.

The Place: San Martín de Porres Parish

San Martín, as it is usually called, is located close to the heart of a big city. Now mainly Hispanic, it has long served as a point of entry for new immigrant groups coming to the United States. Its neighborhood housing is almost 100 years old in some places (and looks it), and spotty attempts at gentrification are evident on a few of the blocks closest to downtown. The parish church is a wonder to behold. Like some graying, wise dowager, the church stands nobly in the midst of the neighborhood, bearing its 100 years proudly. It is a church that welcomes people with tradition and reminders of human presence. On entering, one immediately notices banks of vigil lights flickering before statues of saints. From the wooden pews carved almost 100 years ago by an artisan parishioner to the large, affectionately adorned image of Our Lady of Guadalupe, one sees tangible signs of the love of generations of people of different cultures for this, their place of worship, their church. Here is the holy ground where living saints walk daily.

Rites of Early Childhood

Presentación del Niño

xcitement filled the air. "We're pregnant!" was the way Manuel and Carmen told everyone when they first revealed the good news. Pregnant with life, they were young, hopeful, ready and willing to embrace whatever would be.

Though the nine months passed with relative ease, the last few moments of the pregnancy did not. The excitement of being together at the delivery gave way to the tension of separation as preparations for a caesarean section were made. Silent prayer weaved everyone together. The moment finally broke open as, wrapped in one another's arms, mother, father and newborn child breathed together the air of love and the feeling of relief.

This exciting morning, not quite 40 days from that life-giving event, Manuel, Carmen and their baby, Natividad, would present themselves at church to receive the traditional blessing of God and the sacred oil of beginning from their church brothers and sisters.

This was the third time they had walked this path. The memory of their first experience with Father Kevin was bittersweet. It was bitter in the sense of Kevin's "What does this mean?" "What do we do?" and "Who does what?" questions. Because he didn't have the right answers it seemed that something was lacking. Manuel had become defensive. Father Kevin seemed frustrated and on the verge of saying something he did not mean.

Carlos, the deacon, heard the strained voices and intervened. His calmness cooled the tempers. He explained that the *presentación* was like a preparation ceremony for a bigger event. It was a way of giving thanks to God for this child and introducing the newborn to the people of the parish. Manuel embraced Carlos's explanation, while Kevin tried to understand.

The sweetness was added when Kevin suggested that the signing of the cross and the marking with the oil of catechumens, taken from the preparatory rites of the baptismal ritual, be incorporated in the *presentación*. Carmen's mother later added the traditional Marian consecration. Manuel and Carmen saw these additions as enhancements of their family traditions. The *presentación* would also initiate a series of gatherings with other parents and *padrinos* preparing for the baptism of their children. Each time since that first occasion, Carmen and Manuel have come away with a greater feeling of belonging to the church and to the God who had blessed them.

Pastoral Notes

The rite of presenting a child at the church, *la presentación del niño,* is a Mexican, Mexican American custom stemming from a desire to invoke

divine protection upon the vulnerable newborn and gratitude for a safe childbirth. Pastoral ministers should be aware that a related custom called *echar agua* (literally meaning "to pour water") is practiced by people from Puerto Rico. *Echar agua* appears to be very similar to the rite of emergency baptism because it involves pouring water over a child. However, it is not something done exclusively in the case of need and is considered independent of baptism as a sacrament. The traditional ritual words accompanying the *echar agua* rite pronounced by the person who pours water over the infant reflect its direct relationship to baptism and also to the influence of Spanish Catholicism: "Me lo entregaste moro, y te lo devuelvo cristiano" ("You gave him to me a Moor [that is, a "Moslem"], and I give back to you a Christian"). Because of its more public nature, and because it is clearly a rite preparatory to baptism, the Mexican custom of the presentation of the child seems to offer more possibilities for adapting the initiatory rites in a Hispanic *ambiente.*

This presentation rite is traditionally celebrated at one of two moments in the life of the child. It can be done within 40 days after birth, or it can be a blessing for children who have reached their third birthday. It should be remembered that many of these customs originated in the developing world, where newborns and young children often die. Happily, infant mortality is less a problem in the United States. This custom, however, can still be an important pastoral opportunity to celebrate God's gift of new life — not only within the family but within the larger community. The *presentación* can be a natural occasion for parents to announce the birth of a child to the parish community. Especially with the birth of their first child, this moment can also help mark the beginning of the prebaptismal formation of the parents. The ritual proposed that follows here emphasizes the newborn infant and incorporates the marking with the cross and the anointing of the infant with the oil of catechumens. In this it follows a pattern suggested by the

Rite of Christian Initiation Adults (RCIA), where the rites of initiation take place in a progressive way over time and not in one ritual moment. If this marking and anointing is performed at the time of the *presentación,* there is no need to repeat it at the moment of the celebration of baptism: Originally these rites were separate rituals performed during the adult catechumenate that were telescoped into the infant rite of baptism. The rite appropriately and ideally takes place on a Sunday with the community present and is celebrated after the proclamation of the gospel and the homily.

The *presentación* may also initiate a series of gatherings. Some are more formational and are held in small groups with other parents and *padrinos.* Others are more formal and celebratory and are celebrated with the entire parish community. The excitement of life's new start will be shared and felt by both *familia* and *pueblo* later, when the child is publicly bathed in the waters of baptism. In the time-honored practice of *la entrega,* the *padrinos* would return their godchild back to Manuel and Carmen, bonding themselves to one another for life. Later, at home, after the *fiesta* has become a treasured memory and life has returned to its ordinary passion, the particular kind of excitement would one day return with the announcement, "We're pregnant."

Presentación al Templo de un Niño Dentro de la Misa

Después de la homilía, se invita los padres con sus recién nacidos a acercarse al altar y ubicarse delante de la asamblea.
Celebrante (monición): La vida es el mayor don que hemos recibido de Dios y la vida de los hijos es el signo mayor de la bendición divina para nuestra familia.

Nosotros hemos recibido esos dones, por ellos, venimos para presentar a N. y N. al Señor y Dueño nuestro; queremos que los bendiga y acepte como lo hizo con los niños más cercanos a El en su vida mortal, de manera que puedan ser buenos cristianos en esta vida.
A los padres: Al presentar a su niño/niña hoy día, se comprometen a seguir educándolo(a) en la fe. ¿Aceptan esta obligación que contraen delante de esta asamblea?
Los padres: Sí, aceptamos.

LA SEÑAL DE LA CRUZ

N. y N., la comunidad cristiana los recibe con gran alegría. En su nombre yo les marco con la señal de la cruz; y, en seguida, sus padres y familiares les marcarán con la misma señal de Cristo, el Salvador.

UNCIÓN CON EL ACEITE DE LOS CATECÚMENOS

Celebrante: Por la unción de estos niños, les damos la bienvenida como miembros de la familia de Cristo e iniciamos nuestra jornada unidos a ellos hacia el bautismo.
La unción se hace con el aceite de los catecúmenos a la altura del pecho.
N., te ungimos con el aceite de salvación en el nombre de Cristo, nuestro salvador; que El te fortalezca con su fuerza, que vive y reina por los siglos de los siglos. Amén.

Presentation of a Child
at the Church During Mass

After the homily, parents with their newborns are invited to draw near the altar and stand before the assembly.

Presider: Life is God's greatest gift to us. The life of a newborn child is the family's greatest sign of blessing.

Since we have received the gift of a new life, we come to present N. & N. to the Lord our God. We ask that God bless them and welcome them as Jesus welcomed the little children during his life on this earth, so that they may become good Christians in this life.

To the parents: By presenting a child today, you commit yourselves to continue to form him (her) in the ways of faith. Do you accept this obligation that you affirm in the presence of this assembly?

Parents: Yes, we accept this commitment.

The Sign of the Cross

N., the Christian community welcomes you with great joy. In its name I claim you for Christ our savior by the sign of his cross. I now trace the cross on your foreheads and invite your parents, godparents and relatives to do the same.

Anointing with the Oil of Catechumens

Presider: By anointing these children, we welcome them as members of the family of Christ, and we begin our journey with them toward baptism.

The anointing is done with the oil of the catechumens on the chest.

N., we anoint you with the oil of salvation in the name of Christ, our savior; may he strengthen you with his power, who lives and reigns for ever and ever. Amen.

Al final de la Misa

Consagración y Bendición
a la Virgen María

Celebrante: Santísima Virgen María, Madre de Dios y Madre nuestra, te presentamos a estos niños que Dios ha dado y confiado a tu cuidado y protección. Te los consagramos con todo nuestro corazón, y te los entregamos confiadamente a tu ternura y vigilancia maternal. A sus padres ayúdales a cumplir fielmente sus obligaciones hacia ellos y el compromiso que han contraído delante de Dios. Que su palabra y especialmente con el ejemplo les enseñen a creer y practicar las verdades de la fe, el amor al prójimo y el cumplimiento de la ley de Dios que Cristo nos mostró. Intercede por ellos ante tu Hijo, que vive y reina con el Padre y el Espíritu Santo por los siglos de los siglos. Amén.

At the End of Mass

CONSECRATION TO THE VIRGIN MARY
AND BLESSING

Presider: Most holy virgin Mary, mother of God and our Mother,
we present to you these children that God has given us and
place them in your care and protection. We consecrate them
with our whole heart, and we give them over to your tenderness and maternal love. Help their parents faithfully fulfill the
obligations they have committed themselves to this day in
the presence of God. May their words and especially their
example teach their children to believe and put into practice
the truths of the faith: love of neighbor and faithfulness
to the commandments as Christ has taught us. Intercede for
them, Blessed Mother, with your Son, who lives and reigns
with the Father and the Holy Spirit, now and for ever and
ever. Amen.

Bautismo

Life's new start is shared and felt by both *familia* and *pueblo* when a child is publicly bathed in the waters of baptism. Manuel and Carmen's family felt they belonged to San Martín Parish. Since their first *presentación,* people recognized them around the neighborhood.

This baptismal Sunday they were up early, finishing some last-minute cooking for the *fiesta,* interrupting Jesús and Belén's cartoons with orders to get dressed and gulping down breakfast. It seemed a miracle that they made it to church on time. Carmen had made new friends among the other mothers she had met in the prebaptismal preparation meetings. She enjoyed the special attention their families all received in church. She looked forward to having Jon and Ana as *compadres.* Natividad was their link. It is the custom for the *padrinos* to hold the baby during the actual baptism; at the end of the celebration, in a rite called the *entrega,* Jon and Ana will return Natividad back to Manuel and Carmen, bonding themselves to one another. It all seemed so extraordinarily ordinary.

Pastoral Notes

The meaning of infant baptism becomes more apparent when it is celebrated in the context of a community of faith. Mother, father, godparents, family and community incarnate the faith expressed in the rite for those about to be baptized. This is fitting, since human beings do not encounter Jesus in abstraction but in the family and larger community committed to gospel values. Of capital importance for an effective celebration of the sacrament of baptism, then, is an accurate appreciation of the contours of this community. Questions need to be asked in order to understand and appreciate the context. First, who is this family presenting their child for baptism? Does the couple have family here in the United States, or are they alone in this part of the country? What is their relationship to the surrounding culture(s) of the United States? These and other factors will influence both pre-baptismal instruction and the celebration of the rite of baptism itself.

Compadrazgo

The presider also must be aware of an institution that confirms deeply felt personal relationships within the Hispanic community: *compadrazgo,* or "godparentage." To be a godparent is to be more than someone who simply fulfills an honorary ceremonial task at the moment of baptism. *Compadrazgo* usually involves a solemn commitment to the family as friend, confidant and advisor — and a commitment to become a true "other parent" to the newly baptized child. After the baptism, the parents and godparents will address each other as *compadre* or *comadre* — a term that implies a close and sacred relationship. Because of the very important role of the godparent, it is not unusual for the parents to decide to delay baptism until the godparents can be present. Unlike other cultural communities in which "proxy" godparentage is practiced, this custom is not common with Latinos. Physical presence on this occasion is extremely important. Thus, in addition to the welcome of a young life into new life in Christ, baptism celebrates the family's further growth by means of a spiritual relationship.

Ambiente

In the Hispanic *ambiente,* baptism is the culmination of the many ways in which this community of faith and the domestic church that is the family has embraced and welcomed the newborn. It is most important to remember — in all liturgical celebrations regardless of culture — that involvement of all present is a crucial component of a successful celebration in the Hispanic *ambiente*. Recognition of the presence of the *ancianos*, the grandparents and other elderly relatives, as well as of the younger members of the family, is an important element in the introduction of the rite. Also important is ensuring that all can see and hear. If the number of persons is not unwieldy, the presider is encouraged to follow the ritual movements as found in the rite. There are three "stations" suggested for the celebration of baptism: the welcoming that takes place at the entrance to the church, the procession to the font for baptism, and the move from the font to the altar. These movements tap into the Hispanic sense of drama and participation. They also allow for catechesis about the ritual bath of baptism as the beginning of a journey in the Lord accompanied in the presence of family and community.

Extra attention needs to be given to the moments of welcome and explanation of the rite. Not surprisingly, if the presider shows genuine warmth in welcoming the assembled family and friends and in offering a sincere handshake or *abrazo* in congratulation at the end of the celebration, his credibility and effectiveness will be greatly enhanced. The same is also true if the presider looks for appropriate ways to involve those present in the celebration. The signing with the cross at the beginning of the rite, although suggested for the *presentación*, can also be used here in a more extensive way, especially if there are not many children to be baptized. After having signed the child themselves, the parents can then move through the assembly, starting with the godparents, allowing those present to mark the child with the sign of the cross. Be prepared, however, for a moment of "holy chaos," because people will move spontaneously and noisily in order to come into physical contact with the child. If this signing rite takes place with a large number of families, then the value of shared signing can be preserved by having the families that are next to one another mark each others' children. If the baptism takes place at Sunday Mass, a small number of parishioners from the assembly would mark the child also.

Special ritual attention, of course, must be given to the role of the godparents in order to celebrate and reflect the real nature of their new relationship with the baptizand and the family. One of them could be asked before the rite to read one of the readings or lead the litany of the saints — which would include, of course, the names of the patron saints of all the children to be baptized. At the moment of baptism, the presider should ask the parents to entrust the child to the godparents while staying close to them for the pouring of the water. The *entrega* takes place after the giving of the white garment and the lighted candle, and the celebration of the ephpheta rite, at the blessing. The child is passed from the godparents to the mother for the mother's blessing, from her to the father for the father's blessing, and from him back to the *padrinos*. The traditional *entrega* of the child by the godparents to the parents celebrates the special bond established by the relationship of *compadrazgo*. Finally, grandparents and parents can also be invited to bless the child at the end of the rite and offer a traditional prayer of consecration of their son/daughter to Mary. A sample of this prayer is found at the end of the rite of *presentación*.

It should not be forgotten, however, that the ritual focus of the rite is on the proclamation of faith and the water bath. The spirit of the liturgy promoted by Vatican II calls for lavish use of water to highlight the most important part of the rite. For this reason, baptism by immersion is preferred to the more minimal method of pouring water on the head of the infant.

El bolo

In many Mexican and Mexican American families, it is traditional for the *padrinos* to bring with them to the baptism what is called a *bolo* — a small, loosely wrapped packet of coins (dimes and quarters). At the end of the celebration, those present invite the *padrino* to throw the *bolo* outside the church door to the waiting children and adults. The *bolo* could be interpreted as an expression of the *padrinos'* generosity and also as an expression of their desire to take care of their godchild and their willingness to share the happiness of the moment with everyone present. The pastoral minister's appreciation of this practice offers the opportunity to reflect upon the religious meaning of the *bolo*. During the baptismal preparation class, the *padrinos* might be asked about the significance of the *bolo*. This meaning could then be enlarged to include the responsibility we have as Christians to share our resources with one another and to provide for the material well-being of the poor. In the spirit of the *bolo,* why not invite the parents and *padrinos* to bring canned food for the parish food pantry? These gifts, along with the *bolo,* could be blessed before the final blessing of those present. Recognizing, affirming and integrating the *bolo* into the baptismal liturgy helps those present see this custom as a practical consequence of the profession of faith in Christ and the church.

A Note on Photographs and Photographers

Memory is a constant theme within Hispanic ritual practice. Remembering the way a person is baptized, married and burried is more than an intellectual proposition; it is deeply engraved in the heart. It is understandable that at times adjustments have to be made, but it is important that the core of the ritual remain the same. The memory of a particular sacramental event needs to be shared with the entire family, especially

those who cannot be present. Photographs and videos hold the memory of this religious experience for the family. It is not surprising to see pictures and videos being taken even at wakes and funerals. Unfortunately, taking photographs everyone can enjoy often involves putting the photographer at odds with the presider.

In many ways, photographers are caught between the family's wishes to have memorable photos and the presider's desire to maintain a sacred atmosphere. Not all photographers are professional. Some "moonlight" by taking photos to augment their regular income. When push comes to shove (and sometimes it literally does), the photographer will do what the family wants and apologize to the priest or deacon afterward. Pastoral sensitivity toward the family and toward the photographer's efforts requires understanding and forbearance. However, a good rule of thumb to offer photographers/videographers is that they should never place themselves between the assembly and the liturgical action. Offering to pose for photos after the ceremony itself will often help both the photographer and the family feel that it is less crucial to get every last second of the rite on film during the celebration of the rite itself.

Questions for Reflection

1. What has been your experience of the celebration of baptism?

2. When has the rite been effective?

3. When has it failed to inspire?

4. Popular religion is constantly adapting to new situations. Name a Hispanic custom that has changed due to a new geographical or cultural context. Describe baptismal customs that are important to other cultures.

5. One person's piety is often another person's superstition. What influences a pastoral agent's attitude toward the practices of popular religion?

El Rito del Bautismo de Niños Fuera de la Misa

Bienvenida

A la entrada del templo, el celebrante da una bienvenida calurosa a las familias de los que van a recibir bautismo, por ejemplo:

Mis hermanos y hermanas, bienvenidos a la parroquia de N. Les agradecemos todo lo que han hecho para estar aquí hoy día. Su presencia es una bendición de Dios para todos nosotros y sobre todo para los niños que van a ser acogidos en la familia de Cristo.

Interrogatorio

El celebrante pregunta a los papás de cada niño:

¿Qué nombre quieren darle ustedes a su hijo(a)?

R: Queremos que se llame N.

¿Qué piden a la iglesia de Dios para N.?

R: La gracia del bautismo.

El celebrante puede utilizar otras palabras para este diálogo.

La primera respuesta debe ser dada por alguien diferente a los padres, si las costumres locales les conceden el derecho de nombrar al niño(a).

Ustedes papás, que piden el bautismo para su hijo(a), deben darse cuenta de que contraen la obligación de educarlo en la fe para que sepa guardar los mandamientos divinos: amar a Dios y a su prójimo como Cristo nos enseñó ¿Aceptan esta obligación?

R: Sí, la aceptamos.

El celebrante pregunta a los padrinos:

Y ustedes, padrinos, ¿Están dispuestos a ayudar a los padres de este niño a cumplir con esa obligación?

R: Sí, estamos dispuestos.

Rite of Baptism of Children Outside of Mass

RECEPTION OF THE CHILDREN

At the entrance to the church, the presider warmly greets all present with these or similar words:

My brothers and sisters, welcome to the parish of N.
We sincerely thank you for all you have done to be present
with us here today for this celebration. Your presence is
a blessing for us and especially for the children who will
be welcomed this day into the family of Christ.

INTERROGATION

First the presider questions the parents of each child.

By what name do you wish this community to know your child?
R: N.
What do you ask of God's church for N.?
R: Baptism

The celebrant may choose other words for this dialogue.

The first reply may be given by someone other than the parents if local custom gives them the right to name the child.

You have asked to have your children baptized. In doing so you
are accepting the responsibility of training them in the practice
of the faith. It will be your duty to bring them up to keep God's
commandments as Christ taught us, by loving God and our
neighbor. Do you clearly understand what you are undertaking?
R: We do.

Then the presider turns to the godparents and addresses them in these or similar words:

Godparents, are you ready to help these parents in their duty
as Christian mothers and fathers?
R: We are.

La comunidad cristiana te recibe con gran alegría. En nombre de ella, yo te marco con la señal de la cruz. Y ustedes, papás, padrinos, familiares y amigos, hagan también sobre él/ella la señal de la cruz.

El celebrante traza la señal de la cruz en la frente del niño(a), sin decir nada. Después invita a que hagan lo mismo los demás.

El celebrante invita a los padres, padrinos y demás participantes a dirigirse al lugar de la celebración de la Palabra de Dios. Si las circunstancias lo permiten, se hace una entrada procesional cantando un canto apropiado.

Liturgia de la Palabra

La lecturas

Se invita a uno de los padrinos a leer una lectura que se encuentra en el libro del ritual del bautismo.

Homilía

Oración de los Fieles y Letanía

Se invita a uno de los familiares a anunciar las peticiones y a invocar los nombres de los santos, sobre todo, los patronos de los niños, del templo, del lugar.

Celebrante: Oremos ahora por estos niños que van a ser bautizados, por sus padres y padrinos y por todo el pueblo santo de Dios.

Lector: Para que estos niños, al participar en el misterio de la muerte y resurrección de Cristo, alcancen nueva vida y, por el bautismo, se incorporen a su santa Iglesia. Roguemos al Señor.
R: Te rogamos, Señor.

N. and N. (*or* My dear children), the Christian community welcomes you with great joy. In its name I claim you for Christ our Savior by the sign of his cross. I now trace the cross on your foreheads and invite your parents (and godparents) to do the same.

He signs each child on the forehead, in silence. Then he invites the others present to do the same.

The presider invites the parents, the godparents and the others to take part in the liturgy of the word. If circumstances permit, there is a procession to the place where this will be celebrated, during which a song is sung, for example, Psalm 84: 7, 8.

CELEBRATION OF GOD'S WORD

Readings

A godparent may then be invited to proclaim one of the readings proposed in the Ritual for Baptism.

Homily

INTERCESSIONS (PRAYER OF THE FAITHFUL)

One of the family may be invited to lead the prayer of the faithful and the litany of saints, adding the names of the patrons of the children, the church, the locality.

Presider: My brothers and sisters, let us ask that our Lord Jesus Christ look lovingly on these children who are to be baptized, on the parents and godparents, and on all the baptized.

Lector: By the mystery of your death and resurrection, bathe these children in light, give them the new life of baptism and welcome them into your holy church; let us pray to the Lord. *R:* Lord, hear our prayer.

Lector: Para que el bautismo, la confirmación y la eucaristía los hagan fieles discípulos suyos, que den testimonio del Evangelio en el mundo. Roguemos al Señor.
R: Te rogamos, Señor.

Lector: Para que a través de una vida santa lleguen al Reino de los Cielos. Roguemos al Señor.
R: Te rogamos, Señor.

Lector: Para que los padres y padrinos sean ejemplos de fe viva para estos niños. Roguemos al Señor.
R: Te rogamos, Señor.

Lector: Para que Dios guarde siempre en su amor a estas familias. Roguemos al Señor.
R: Te rogamos, Señor.

Lector: Para que renueve en todos la gracia del bautismo. Roguemos al Señor.
R: Te rogamos, Señor.

Santa María, Madre de Dios
R: Ruega por nosotros.

San José, esposo de la Virgen
R: Ruega por nosotros.

San Juan Bautista
R: Ruega por nosotros.

Santos Apóstoles Pedro y Pablo
R: Rueven por nosotros.

San N. y N (patronos de los niños)
R: Rueven por nosotros.

Todos los santos y santas
R: Rueven por nosotros.

Leader: Through baptism, confirmation, and eucharist, make them your faithful followers and witnesses to your gospel; let us pray to the Lord.
R: Lord, hear our prayer.

Leader: Lead them by a holy life to the joys of God's kingdom; let us pray to the Lord.
R: Lord, hear our prayer.

Leader: Make the lives of their parents and godparents examples of faith to inspire these children; let us pray to the Lord.
R: Lord, hear our prayer.

Leader: Keep their families always in your love; let us pray to the Lord.
R: Lord, hear our prayer.

Leader: Renew the grace of our baptism in each one of us; let us pray to the Lord.
R: Lord, hear our prayer.

Holy Mary, Mother of God
R: Pray for us.

Saint Joseph, husband of the Virgin
R: Pray for us.

Saint John the Baptist
R: Pray for us.

Saint Peter and Saint Paul
R: Pray for us.

Saints N. & N. (patrons of the baptizands)
R: Pray for us.

All holy men and women.
R: Pray for us.

LITURGIA DEL SACRAMENTO

Bendición del Agua e Invocación a Dios

Si la fuente bautismal está en otro lugar, se organiza allá la procesión. Se puede cantar algo apropiado.

Al llegar a la fuente bautismal, el celebrante recuerda a los presentes, con breves palabras, el plan de Dios, quien ha querido santificarnos por medio del agua.

Dios comunica su vida a los creyentes por medio del sacramento del agua. Avivemos nuestra fe y pidamos todos unidos que estos niños renazcan por el agua y el Espíritu Santo.

Te bendecimos, Padre lleno de bondad, porque has hecho brotar en nosotros la vida nueva de hijos tuyos que mana de la fuente bautismal.
R: Bendito seas por siempre, Señor.

Tú, que por el agua y el Espíritu unes en un solo pueblo a todos los que son bautizados en tu Hijo Jesucristo.
R: Bendito seas por siempre, Señor.

Tú, que nos haces libres por el Espíritu de tu amor que infundes en nuestros corazones, que gocemos de paz.
R: Bendito seas por siempre, Señor.

Tú, que eliges a los bautizados para que anuncien alegremente el Evangelio de Cristo en todas las naciones.
R: Bendito seas por siempre, Señor.

Dígnate ahora bendecir + esta agua, con la cual van a ser bautizados tus hijos e hijas, a quienes has llamado al baño que da nueva vida en la fe de tu Iglesia, para que posean la vida eterna. Por Cristo nuestro Señor.
R: Amén.

CELEBRATION OF THE SACRAMENT

Blessing of the Water

If the baptistry is located outside the church or is not within view of the congregation, all go there in procession.

When they come to the font, the presider briefly reminds the assembly of the wonderful work of God, whose plan it is to sanctify human beings, body and soul, through water. He may use these or similar words:

My dear brothers and sisters, God uses the sacrament of water to give divine life to those who believe. Let us turn to God and ask him to pour the gift of life from this font on the children God has chosen.

Presider: God of mercy, through these waters of baptism you filled us with new life as your very own children.
R: Blessed be God forever.

Presider: From all who are baptized in water and the Holy Spirit, you have formed one people, united in your Son Jesus Christ.
R: Blessed be God forever.

Presider: You have set us free and filled our hearts with the Spirit of your love, that we may live in your peace.
R: Blessed be God forever.

Presider: You call those who have been baptized to announce the Good News of Jesus Christ to people everywhere.
R: Blessed be God forever.

Presider: You have called your children, N., N., to this cleansing water and new birth that by sharing the faith of your church they might have eternal life. Bless + this water in which they will be baptized. We ask this in the name of Christ our Lord.
R: Amen.

*Pero durante el tiempo pascual, si hay a la mano agua bautismal ya
bendita, el celebrante omite la última parte de la bendición precedente,
"Dígnate ahora bendecir . . . ", y concluye de esta manera:*
> Por el misterio de esta agua bendita, haz nacer de nuevo
> espiritualmente a tus hijos y a tus hijas, a quienes has llamado
> a este baño que se administra en la fe de tu Iglesia, para que
> posean la vida eterna. Por Cristo nuestro Señor.
>
> *R:* Amén.

RENUNCIA Y PROFESIÓN DE FE

Celebrante: Estimados padres y padrinos, en esta celebración
de la Iglesia, Dios va a mostrarnos su amor por medio de su
Espíritu al dar una vida nueva a sus hijos, que hoy renacerán a
la vida de la gracia.

Para esto, ustedes deben enseñarles la doctrina de
Cristo, principalmente con el buen ejemplo, para que la gracia
que hoy van a recibir pueda desarrollarse y aumentar cada
día más.

Si es verdad que ustedes quieren cumplir con esta obligación de padres y padrinos, renuncien al pecado y proclamen
su fe en Jesucristo, que es la fe de la Iglesia en la que sus hijos
van a ser bautizados. Por eso les pregunto:

¿Renuncian al pecado para que no se pierda jamás la vida
divina que han recibido en su bautismo?

R: Sí creo.

¿Renuncian a Satanás y todas sus obras que encaminan
siempre al mal y a la destrucción?

R: Sí creo.

¿Renuncian ustedes a las seducciones, a las injusticias,
a la guerra, al egoísmo y a los pecados del tener, del poder
y del placer?

R: Sí creo.

If the baptismal water has already been blessed, the celebrant omits this last prayer and says:

You have called your children, N., N., to this cleansing water that they may share in the faith of your church and have eternal life. By the mystery of this consecrated water, lead them to a new and spiritual birth. We ask this through Christ our Lord.
R: Amen.

RENUNCIATION OF SIN AND PROFESSION OF FAITH

Presider: Dear parents and godparents: You have come here to present these children for baptism. By water and the Holy Spirit they are to receive the gift of new life from God, who is love.

On your part, you must make it your constant care to bring them up in the practice of the faith. See that the divine life which God gives them is kept safe from the poison of sin, to grow always stronger in their hearts.

If your faith makes you ready to accept this responsibility, renew now the vows of your own baptism. Renounce sin; profess your faith in Christ Jesus. This is the faith of the church. This is the faith in which these children are about to be baptized.

Do you renounce sin, so as never to lose the divine life that your have received in baptism?
R: I do.

Do you renounce Satan and all his works that lead to evil and destruction?
R: I do.

Do you renounce injustice, war, selfishness and all sins of materialism, power and pleasure?
R: I do.

¿Creen en Dios Padre todopoderoso, creador del cielo
y de la tierra?
R: Sí creo.

¿Creen en Jesucristo, su único Hijo, Señor nuestro, que nació
de Santa María Virgen, padeció, fue sepultado, resucitó
de entre los muertos y está sentado a la derecha del Padre?
R: Sí creo.

¿Creen en el Espíritu Santo, en la santa Iglesia católica,
en la comunión de los santos, en el perdón de los pecados,
en la resurrección de los muertos y en la vida eterna?
R: Sí creo.

Esta es nuestra fe. Esta es la fe de la Iglesia, que nos gloriamos
de profesar, en Jesucristo nuestro Señor.
R: Amén.

BAUTISMO

*El celebrante invita a la familia para que se acerque a la fuente
bautismal, y pregunta a los papás y a los padrinos:*
¿Quieren que N. sea bautizado(a) en esta fe de la Iglesia,
que todos juntos acabamos de profesar?
R: Sí queremos.

Se entrega el niño a los padrinos.
En seguida el celebrante bautiza al niño, diciendo,
N., YO TE BAUTIZO EN EL NOMBRE DEL PADRE,
Derrama el agua sobre la cabeza del niño o lo sumerge
Y DEL HIJO,
Por segunda vez derrama agua sobre la cabeza del niño o lo sumerge
Y DEL ESPIRITU SANTO.
Por tercera vez derrama agua sobre la cabeza del niño o lo sumerge.

Do you believe in God, the Father almighty, Creator of heaven and earth?

R: I do.

Do you believe in Jesus Christ, his only Son, our Lord, who was born of the Virgin Mary, was crucified, died and was buried, rose from the dead and is now seated at the right hand of the Father?

R: I do.

Do you believe in the Holy Spirit, the holy catholic Church, the communion of saints, the forgiveness of sins, the resurrection of the body and life everlasting?

R: I do.

This is our faith. This is the faith of the church. We are proud to profess it, in Christ Jesus our Lord.

R: Amen.

BAPTISM

The presider invites the first of the families to the font. Using the name of each individual child, he questions the parents and godparents.

Is it your will that N. should be baptized in the faith of the church, which we have all professed with you?

R: It is.

The child is given to the godparents.
He baptizes the child, saying,

N., I BAPTIZE YOU IN THE NAME OF THE FATHER,

He immerses the child or pours water on the child

AND OF THE SON,

He immerses the child or pours water on the child a second time

AND OF THE HOLY SPIRIT.

He immerses the child or pours water on the child a third time. He asks the same question and performs the same action for each child.

Unción con el Santo Crisma

Celebrante: Dios todopoderoso, Padre de nuestro Señor Jesucristo, que te ha librado del pecado y te ha dado la nueva vida
por el agua y el Espíritu Santo, te unja con el crisma de la
salvación para que, incorporado a su pueblo, seas para siempre
miembro de Cristo Sacerdote, de Cristo Profeta y de Cristo Rey.
R: Amén.

En seguida, el celebrante unge con el crisma a los niños en la coronilla.

Imposición de la Vestidura Blanca

N., ya has sido transformado en una nueva criatura y te has
revestido de Cristo. Que esta vestidura blanca sea para ti
el símbolo de tu nueva dignidad de cristiano. Con los consejos
y ejemplos de tus familiares, consérvala sin mancha hasta
la vida eterna.
R: Amén.

Entrega de la Vela Encendida

El papá o el padrino enciende la vela del cirio pascual.
Celebrante: Reciban la luz de Cristo. A ustedes, padres y
padrinos, se les confía el cuidado de esta luz, a fin de que este
niño, que ha sido iluminado por Cristo, camine siempre como
hijo de la luz y, si persevera en la fe, pueda salir al encuentro
del Señor con todos los santos cuando venga el final de los
tiempos.

ANOINTING WITH CHRISM

Presider: God the Father of our Lord Jesus Christ has freed you
from sin, given you a new birth by water and the Holy Spirit,
and welcomed you into his holy people. He now anoints you
with the chrism of salvation. As Christ was anointed Priest,
Prophet, and King, so may you live always as members of his
body, sharing everlasting life.
R: Amen.

*Next, the presider anoints each child on the crown of the head with
chrism, in silence.*

CLOTHING WITH WHITE GARMENT

N., you have become a new creation and have clothed yourselves
in Christ. See in this white garment the outward sign of our
Christian dignity. With your family and friends to help you by
word and example, bring that dignity unstained into the
everlasting life of heaven.
R: Amen.

LIGHTED CANDLE

The father or godfather lights the child's candle from the Paschal candle.
Presider: Receive the light of Christ. Parents and godparents,
this light is entrusted to you to be kept burning brightly. These
children of yours have been enlightened by Christ. They are
to walk always as children of the light. May they keep the flame
of faith alive in their hearts. When the Lord comes, may they
go out to meet him with all the saints in the heavenly kingdom.

EFETA

El celebrante toca con el dedo pulgar los oídos y la boca de los niños(as):
El Señor Jesús, que hizo oír a los sordos y hablar a los mudos,
te conceda, a su tiempo, escuchar su palabra y profesar la fe,
para alabanza y gloria de Dios Padre.

CONCLUSIÓN DEL RITO

Si el bautismo no se celebró en el presbiterio, se hace una procesión al altar, durante la cual se lleva encendida la vela de los bautizados.

PADRE NUESTRO

El celebrante, de pie ante el altar, se dirige a los papás, a los padrinos y a todos los presentes, con estas o parecidas palabras:
Hermanos y hermanas: estos niños que han renacido por el
bautismo, y que ya se llaman N. y N., y son hijos de Dios,
recibirán la plenitud del Espíritu Santo en la confirmación
y, cuando se acerquen al altar del Señor, participarán de la
mesa de su sacrificio y llamarán Padre a Dios, en medio
de la asamblea cristiana. Ahora nosotros, en su nombre, con el
espíritu de hijos adoptivos de Dios, que todos hemos recibido,
oremos juntos como el Señor nos enseñó a orar.

Y todos dicen juntamente con el celebrante:
Padre Nuestro . . .

Las madres reciben sus hijos de los padrinos.
El Señor Dios todopoderoso, que por su Hijo nacido de la
Virgen María alegra a las madres cristianas con la esperanza de
la vida eterna, que ha hecho brillar sobre sus hijos, les bendiga
a ustedes madres de estos niños, que se sientan agradecidas

EPHETHA, OR PRAYER OVER EARS AND MOUTH

The presider touches the ears and mouth of each child with his thumb, saying:

The Lord Jesus made the deaf hear and the mute speak. May he soon touch your ears to receive his word, and your mouth to proclaim his faith, to the praise and glory of God the Father.

CONCLUSION OF THE RITE

Next there is a procession to the altar, unless the baptism was performed in the sanctuary. The lighted candles are carried for the children.

LORD'S PRAYER

The presider stands in front of the altar and addresses the parents, the godparents and the whole assembly with these or similar words:

Dearly beloved, these children have been reborn in baptism. They are now called children of God, for so indeed they are. In confirmation they will receive the fullness of God's Spirit. In holy communion they will share the banquet of Christ's sacrifice, calling God their Father in the midst of the Church. In their name, in the Spirit of our common adoption, let us pray together in the words our Lord has given us:

All present join the presider in saying:

Our Father . . .

The mothers are then given their children.

God the Father, through his Son, the Virgin Mary's child, has brought joy to all Christian mothers, as they see the hope of eternal life shine on their children. May God bless the mothers of these children. They now thank God for the gift

por haberlos recibido, para que permanezcan siempre con
ellos en continua acción de gracias, en Jesucristo nuestro Señor.
R: Amén.

Los padres reciben sus hijos de las madres.
El Señor todopoderoso, que nos ha dado la vida terrenal y
la celestial, les bendiga a ustedes padres de estos niños, para
que juntamente con sus esposas sean los primeros que,
de palabra y obra, den testimonio de la fe ante sus hijos,
en Jesucristo nuestro Señor.
R: Amén.

Los padrinos reciben de nuevo sus ahijados de los padres.
El Señor todopoderoso, que nos ha hecho renacer a la vida
eterna por el agua y el Espíritu Santo, bendiga abundantemente
a todos ustedes, los aquí presentes, para que siempre y en todas
partes sean miembros vivos de su pueblo, y les dé su paz,
en Jesucristo nuestro Señor.
R: Amén.

La Entrega de los Niños

Los padrinos devuelven el niño (la niña) a sus padres, diciendo:
Compadre y comadre, aquí les entregamos a nuestro ahijado
que de la Iglesia salió con los santos sacramentos y el agua
que recibió. Se llama N.

Los padres reciben los niños, diciendo:
Recibimos la prenda amada, que ha salido de las aguas de
la vida y que ha recibido los santos sacramentos.

of their children. May they be one with them in thanking
him forever in heaven, in Christ Jesus our Lord.
R: Amen.

The fathers are then given their children.
God is the giver of all life, human and divine. May he bless
the fathers of these children. With their wives they will be the
first teachers of their children in the ways of faith. May they
also be the best of teachers, bearing witness to the faith by what
they say and do, in Christ Jesus our Lord.
R: Amen.

The godparents hold their godchildren.
By God's gift through water and the Holy Spirit, we are reborn
to everlasting life. In his goodness, may he continue to pour
out his blessing upon all present, who are his sons and daughters. May he make you always, wherever you may be, faithful
members of his holy people. May he send his peace upon
all who are gathered here, in Christ Jesus our Lord.
R: Amen.

LA ENTREGA

The godparents then give the children back to the parents saying:
Compadre and *comadre,* here we return to you our godchild
who has come forth from the life-giving waters of baptism and
will continue to grow in the sacraments of the church. His/her
name is N.

And the parents respond:
We claim you again, our beloved child, with gratitude and
thanks; you have come forth from the life-giving waters
of baptism and will continue to grow in the sacraments of
the church.
R: Amen.

BENDICIÓN DE LOS ANCIANOS

Se acercan los ancianos de la familia para bendecir a los recién bautizados en su manera tradicional.

BENEDICIÓN Y DESPEDIDA

Luego, prosigue el ministro:

La bendición de Dios todopoderoso, Padre, Hijo y Espíritu Santo, descienda sobre ustedes ahora y siempre.

R: Amén.

Hermanos y hermanas, vayamos en paz.

R: Demos gracias a Dios.

Todos se abrazan. Después, se puede llevar a los niños al altar de la Virgen Santísima. Para una oración apropiada, vea el ejemplo al final del rito de la presentación del niño o se puede cantar un himno mariano.

BLESSING BY THE ELDERS

The grandparents and other older relatives then come forward and bless the newly baptized children in the traditional manner.

BLESSING AND DISMISSAL

The presider then continues:
And may almighty God, the Father, and the Son, and Holy
Spirit, bless you.
R: Amen.

Let us go in peace.
R: Thanks be to God.

After the blessing, all may sing the song of the Blessed Virgin Mary, the Magnificat or a traditional Marian hymn. Where there is the practice of bringing baptized infants to the altar of the Blessed Virgin Mary, this custom is observed, if appropriate. For a blessing/consecration prayer, please see an example at the end of the Rite for the Presentation of the Child, pages 28 and 29.

Rites of Later Childhood and Adolescence

The Celebration of First Communion

hy is it that parents seem to relive their childhoods through their children? Parent sacramental preparation meetings and first communion Mass often are lightning rods for many unresolved personal, familial and parochial issues. The differences between the parish staff and the participating first communion families become very apparent. Vatican II's liturgical goal of noble simplicity seems to clash head-on with lavish religious practices. Father Kevin was glad that first communion only came once a year. This year, however, he was convinced he needed to try a new approach.

Everyone had their own way. Everyone wanted their own way. Everyone was angry that they were not going to get their way. It was enough to make a person wish for the days when the pastor's words were unquestioned law, and he had *his* way. So went Father Kevin's morning meditation the day after he had initiated a dialogue with the parents of the first communion class. A priest friend of Kevin's had persuaded him to find out what the people wanted but also what the Hispanic traditional customs were that they followed. It was a learning experience that Kevin did not want to repeat for a long time. Yet, he had to admit, he did learn how important this event was and also the amazing number of traditional family customs associated with first communion. Now he prayed for the wisdom of Solomon.

As Father Kevin meditated, Manuel's morning tirade focused on a common problem, and, as usual, he and Kevin were at different ends of the spectrum. Belén's first communion clothes, prayer book, rosary, lighted candle, photographer, scapular, holy cards and *padrinos* were all non-negotiables to the family. Each child's first communion was unique. "It should be a memorable experience for her and for us," he told Carmen, who busied herself with other matters. She knew that a compromise would eventually be worked out — but not at this morning's meeting. There would be more preparation meetings, and all of this would be discussed again.

San Martín church never looked so good or so proud in the early afternoon's warm spring light. It was as if you could see the first communion processions of a hundred afternoons before. The twelve o'clock Mass began with the first communicants' entrance. They carefully held lighted candles. The girls were dressed in white while the boys sported a haphazard array of dark colored pants and white shirts with special arm bands. Some of the boys even had suits. The communicants ran the range from eight to almost fifteen years of age. They looked good. They looked proud.

The arrangements for the celebration had been negotiated in light of a fortuitous insight that Father Kevin had at one of the parent meetings. People wanted their customs to be respected, but many did not know the origin of many of the religious practices associated with first communion — and they were completely unfamiliar with other traditions that came from different areas in Latin America. So why not adjust the information shared in the parent meetings to use each of these first communion traditions as the starting place for discussing central aspects of the eucharist? The parish staff developed a process of catechesis that was culturally sensitive, theologically sound and linked with ritual prayer.

Kevin sought out Manuel, one of his more vocal critics. At first Manuel balked, but gradually he saw the wisdom of the idea. He even volunteered to help in any way he could with the parent meetings — and so it happened. The parent discussions helped Kevin to offer ideas about the church's liturgical tradition of the eucharist as well as gain further insight into his Hispanic parishioners' language of prayer. Manuel and Carmen, as well as the other parents, also developed a greater appreciation and love for the eucharist. The Sunday after each meeting, the children were blessed and presented with the different religious symbols that would be used on the day of their first communion. San Martín parish fashioned a new yet traditional first communion celebration that became a parish tradition.

Pastoral Notes

It is obvious to even the most casual observer that the first communion of a child is an important celebration in a Latino family. But while the religious significance of the eucharist is a primary focus for the event, its familial and social dimensions play an even more crucial role than in many Euro-American families. In the Hispanic community, first communion is surrounded by many customs handed down from one generation to the next. Some of these traditions are unique to a given Hispanic culture or even to a specific family and are especially significant since they serve as a means of linking the generations and of maintaining contact with the "old country." Many of the religious symbols associated with first communion are shared by all Hispanic groups: prayer books, rosaries, scapulars, candles. White veils and dresses for the girls and ribbons or armbands for the boys are also common "extras" for first communion. While they may seem very secondary, if these elements are ignored or dismissed by pastoral ministers, the catechesis surrounding the event may be jeopardized.

Any effective parish approach to first communion must be sensitive to the larger extended family context in which this rite is celebrated and to the Latino traditions that are associated with first communion. While it may seem to be a case of misplaced priorities, it is not uncommon for families to want to postpone the first communion of a child because they do not have enough money for new clothes or because they cannot provide a respectable *fiesta* after the event. While pastoral ministers may rightly criticize this delay, it is important to keep in mind that in a Hispanic context, these sacramental celebrations never take place disconnected from human relationships. From a pastoral point of view, not only the child's preparation for the first reception of the eucharist but also the larger set of interpersonal ties that link a child to his/her world also need to be attended to and celebrated in order for the catechesis to make sense — not only to the child but to everyone else as well. It is also important to be aware that, as in the celebration of baptism, *compadres* can also play an important role — especially in helping the family pay for the extra expenses that a celebration of this nature often entails.

For this reason, the vignette presented here suggests a way of approaching first communion preparation that involves the parents and godparents with their children in a process that uses the Hispanic religious symbols as the starting point for catechesis on the eucharist. Rather than inadvertently imposing an approach that risks being disconnected from the Latino cultural context, moving from Hispanic customs associated with this celebration to the broader theological issues offers a method that has two important advantages. First, inviting parents and godparents to speak about their own customs — how they experienced their own first communions — creates a more hospitable *ambiente* and affirms their cultural identity and religious traditions. It also highlights their own role as the first evangelizers of their children by encouraging them to share their own expressions of faith. It is quite possible that not everyone will be able to explain all the historical and theological background of their customs. For this reason, catechists and the pastoral team will have to be prepared to supplement these initial explanations. Also, because the customs sometimes vary from one group to another, it is important to do some homework by asking some reliable members of the parish about their experience of first communion. It is not necessary to know everything ahead of time, of course; the dialogue with the parents is also designed to be a real sharing of experiences among the parishioners and the hosts of the discussion. The fact that it is the parents who speak first and the pastoral ministers who listen shows respect for the parental role that will be modeled in future encounters.

This approach also has the advantage of using the preparatory sessions with the children and parents as a time of communal prayer. It is in this context that the religious symbols drawn from Hispanic culture are presented. The blessing and giving of the religious symbols in the context of prayer — parents with their children in the presence of the Sunday assembly — also grounds the preparation in an experience of worship that goes beyond the immediate or extended family and involves the larger parish. It prepares both the children and the parents for what is to come and helps to keep the focus on the religious dimensions of the celebration while not neglecting the cultural and familial context in which it is celebrated.

Another traditional expectation on the part of many Latinos in the preparation of their children for first communion is first confession/reconciliation. Today, in many parishes throughout the United States, there is a growing uneasiness about *requiring* sacramental reconciliation before first communion, due to the difficulty many seven-year-olds have in really understanding issues of sin, culpability and satisfaction. For this reason we will discuss the sacrament of reconciliation in a later section of this chapter that deals with youth ministry to adolescents in the context of the *Quince Años* celebration.

Questions for Reflection

1. What is the parish experience of preparing and receiving first communion? How has this experience changed within the last number of years?

2. Popular religion stresses relationships with the saints through engaging in particular devotions and prayers. What are the family prayer patterns that are taught at home? Can any of these appropriately find their way into Sunday worship so as to link domestic and liturgical prayer?

3. What are the family meal practices of the local community? Is prayer before meals practiced and encouraged?

4. How do the meal customs of the U.S. and Hispanic communities influence one another?

A Catechetical Prayer Session

The variety of religious symbols attached to first communion is dependent upon family, regional and national customs. This first session seeks to identify these symbols, affirm their religious value and reflect theologically on their meaning for the family and the parish. Though others may surface, our experience has been that the Hispanic symbols associated with first communion are centered around *padrinos,* prayer book, rosary, scapular of Our Lady of Mount Carmel, special first communion clothing and candles. In the spirit of Vatican II, it would also be appropriate to add a children's edition of the Bible to this list. The adults are the focus of these sessions, since the purpose of these encounters is to help them share their faith and introduce Hispanic religious customs to their children or godchildren. Each meeting will end with communal prayer, with both adults and children present, in a style that can be easily repeated at home on a daily basis.

The team that facilitates these meetings could be composed of members of the pastoral staff (the director of religious education, catechists) as well as parents from the parish (such as Manuel and Carmen in our vignette). During the course of this first evening, presuppositions need to be checked out, such as the place of the family meal in the daily routine of the children; that families have a table that they can all gather around; that every family has a readable edition of the Bible; that the family regularly attends Mass; that both parents live together and are present to their children.

We have noticed that these meetings often give rise to other questions regarding the changes in the church, differences in neighboring parish policies and pastoral issues such as marrying in the church, annulments and divorce. These concerns need to be handled with sensitivity and discretion.

Convivencia means "sharing life" among family and friends and is used to speak about gatherings that emphasize interpersonal sharing. Food and drink in the context of a *convivencia* is always readily available and for this reason has eucharistic overtones. In providing a Hispanic *ambiente* of hospitality, the team needs to create an atmosphere of "sharing life" during these sessions. In order to do this, members of the team need to function as hosts, welcoming the parents and their children and inviting them to the refreshment table. An *altarcito* (literally a "little altar" commonly found in Hispanic homes) needs to be set up in the meeting room to serve as a visual point of reference for the prayer. It should highlight first communion symbols of home and church. Providing recorded music in the background as the people gather is another way to help create an *ambiente* more conducive to real *convivencia*.

First Session: Preparing the Ground

The pastor or other member of the parish pastoral team begins the meeting by welcoming the parents, godparents and children and by presenting the first communion team. A simple opening prayer consisting of a scripture reading, blessing of water and sprinkling of those gathered connects this moment to baptism. The children are led in procession to their classrooms by the catechists while the parents and godparents remain.

The person(s) facilitating the session should welcome those assembled in these or similar words:

Friends, thank you for being here. Our presence this evening is a special gift to our children. We seek to learn from one another and to share our reflections with you about first communion. Since our children were baptized, we have been their first teachers in the ways of faith. We know that many of you have already taught them prayers to the Virgin Mary and to the saints, how to make the sign of the cross and about the presence of Jesus in the eucharist. They are now taking their next steps in a long journey of faith. This is the journey that leads to the parish family table, where all of us receive Christ's body and blood. That is why we are here: to walk with them to the Lord's table. In a moment you will be asked to form small groups of eight to ten people, introduce yourselves and then answer the questions that are being distributed. A member of the team will be part of each group as an active participant. Afterward, we will be called back together to reflect on our answers.

What do you remember from your first communion?

What do you want your child to remember about his/her first communion?

After the break, the facilitator receives reports from the various groups that have been summarized on large pages of newsprint and then taped to the wall for all to see. The facilitator responds, making the following points:

How much our answers resemble one another! How much our memories of nervousness correspond to the emotions of our children. They are very excited about making their first communion. It is plain to see that religious gifts and family customs are very important. Some of you still have your first communion rosary and prayer book. These things keep that special day alive for us. Our future meetings will focus on the meaning of these special gifts. You will be asked to bring the prayer books, rosaries, candles and Bibles to three Sunday Masses prior to first communion, where these religious gifts and your children will be blessed. All of us are on a journey of faith with our children. These meetings, these blessings, are steps in the journey to the parish table of the Lord — the altar of our church. Around this table we are all family. Around this table everyone is welcome. Around this table of word and sacrament God nourishes us. During this week, we ask you to spend some time with your children telling them the story of your own first communion. Ask them what they are learning in class. Tell them you are glad that they will be making their first communion. Let them know that they are becoming members of a bigger family — our parish family. Finally, we have noticed that sometimes people have personal questions. Please feel free to approach one of the members of the pastoral staff after our prayer.

The children then return to their families, and the candles of the altarcito are lit. The facilitator or religious education director invites everyone to pray.

Leader:
(Everyone makes the sign of the cross)
Glory to the Father, and to the Son, and to the Holy Spirit,
as it was in the beginning, is now, and ever shall be,
world without end. Amen.
God's blessing be with you.
All: And also with you.
Leader: Let us pray.
    Blessed are you, God of all creation.
    You bless our family table with the bread of life.
    May we become food that satisfies the hungry heart.
    We ask this through Christ our Lord.
All: Amen.
Reader: "Jesus said: I am the living bread come down from heaven. If anyone eats this bread, they will live forever" (John 6:51).
Leader: Taking the words of Jesus to heart, let us join hands in prayer in the words that he has taught us.
All: Our Father . . .
Leader: Asking for the intercession of the Virgin Mary, we pray:
All: Hail Mary, full of grace . . .

Leader: In many families, the custom of greeting by kissing the hand of a parent, godparent and grandparent is still observed. In closing, let us now kiss one another's hand and mark each other with the sign of the cross.

After this has been done:

Leader: Let us go forth to love and serve the Lord and one another.

All: Thanks be to God.

The team members take their place at the door, saying good-bye to the families as they leave.

Confirmation Memories

Confirmation is a dilemma for the church and therefore for many families. The various theologies and ongoing discussions about the "correct" age for its celebration continue to be sources of much debate in the church in the United States. This is uniquely felt within the Hispanic community. There are a variety of opinions as to the most appropriate age for confirmation. One particular influence shaping the current practice is that most Hispanic young people born in the United States do not attend Catholic schools and are not enrolled in religious education programs. They are thereby left outside the fold of Catholic confirmation practice. This becomes most keenly evident when the sacrament of marriage is being planned. "Catch-up" programs for Hispanic young adults still loom on the horizon. Manuel and Carmen's family add another facet to the diversity of the Hispanic experience of confirmation.

Manuel reminisced about his first communion. He was seven years old, dressed in a white shirt, white pants, brown tie, and brown and white sandals. It was a good day because he didn't get dirty beforehand. What had always struck him as odd and even funny was the day the teacher told his first communion class that the older children were being confirmed. Confirmation was a big word to a seven-year-old. He and his classmates were being told this information usually reserved for older children because they too were going to be confirmed. Apparently, the confirmation class was not big enough for the bishop, and so they were recruited to fill in the ranks. "As long as you know Jesus, you will be fine," said the teacher. The confirmation ceremony gave them a special feeling of being grown-up, though it came and went with barely a thought. Manuel asked his wife what she remembered most about her confirmation.

Saturday morning religious education classes had been part of Carmen's routine since her first communion. "At first I thought it was a drag," she said. And what child wouldn't feel robbed of their Saturday mornings? She remembered that by the time she was in eighth grade, the Saturday classes were actually fun-filled, positive experiences. She considered herself fortunate for two reasons. First, her mother encouraged her to keep attending class by being interested in what she learned. During the changes in the church, as they were commonly called, Carmen was one of the main sources of information for her mother. Second, the program was run by a religious sister who had a gift for making learning a creative and fun experience. Carmen had to admit that she liked church.

Carmen's confirmation was standard by all outward appearances, but it had a real difference. This celebration marked the first time that the public school religious education program and the regular parish school children were intermingled. There had been some parental complaints about this new practice, but the parish team stood its ground. Carmen became more aware of outward appearances and inner beliefs.

When the time came for Carmen and Manuel's oldest son, Jesús, to be confirmed, an amazing thing happened. He had gone to all the classes with the eighth grade, done all the work, even attended the preparation retreat, and then decided *not* to be confirmed. Manuel, Carmen and Father Kevin had all spoken to Jesús at different times, but he remained firm in his decision to delay his confirmation. His reason was simple. He had taken very much to heart what he had been taught about the seriousness of making a decision to live his faith. He had struggled with teenage questions of what he believed and what he questioned. He had come to the conclusion that he was not ready, not mature enough, not old enough to take so serious a step. He wanted time. He asked them to respect his decision to search in his own way. He was 17, almost 18, when he began thinking again about confirmation.

Belén had the unique experience of almost being confirmed as a baby. Shortly after her baptism, Carmen and Manuel made their annual pilgrimage to their "motherland." They went to Mexico to visit Manuel's family. While they were showing the pictures of Belén's baptism to one of Manuel's aunts, she asked, "When would Belén be confirmed?" Responding that the United States practice was to confirm children when they were older, they were reminded that they were now in Mexico, where the practice was to confirm babies and small children. Why not take advantage of this and allow Manuel's family the privilege of confirming Belén? It was a delicate question that required a diplomatic answer. In the silence that ensued, Manuel's aunt noted their hesitancy. She excused herself in order to bring in some refreshments, never returning to the question.

Natividad's first year in an all-girl Catholic high school was a breakthrough. She was the first to attend a Catholic school. There was a hint of parental protection disguised in the notion that she would do better here than elsewhere. But she didn't seem to mind. In the first-year orientation program for new students, she and 20 others had indicated that they were in need of one of the sacraments. During the year they would form a special religion class that would prepare them for the sacrament they lacked. In this way, Nati made her confirmation at the end of her first year of high school.

Pastoral Notes

The sacrament of confirmation has had a rather checkered history in the church at large, but especially in Latin America. For centuries, maintaining a practice common in Spain since the Middle Ages, a sign was posted on the door of the local cathedral announcing that the bishop, at a certain date and time, would confirm all who needed this sacrament. Preparation for the sacrament was judged unnecessary, given the Catholic culture in which the confirmands were being raised and given the fact that confirmation was long regarded as a simple complement to baptism — a way the bishop exercised his role and oversight in the initiation of new members into the church.

Even today in many parts of Latin America, the age for confirmation is quite young. Infants and young children are regularly confirmed. This may seem strange to many in the United States, but this is really the more traditional discipline regarding the sacrament. Confirmation never historically functioned in Latin America as a rite of passage marking "a mature affirmation of the faith." It simply served as a completion of baptism and a prelude to first communion, reflecting the traditional order in which the sacraments of initiation are received. Of course, this was also the case even in the United States during the last century. This traditional way of understanding confirmation was inadvertently altered by a decree by the Congregation of Rites, *Quam singulari* (1910), approved by Pope Pius X, that sought to promote earlier and more frequent access to the eucharist by young children. For this reason, the age for first communion was lowered to "the age of reason" and the conferral of confirmation was delayed until a later date. This led to a reappraisal of the theology of confirmation, which became more centered on a strengthening and individual appropriation of the faith by young people. The new discipline was wholeheartedly embraced in Europe and North America but was much harder to implement in Latin America, where there were fewer bishops and where greater physical distances made travel difficult.

The fact that confirmation is being conferred at various ages around the United States indicates that there is not yet a consensus about the meaning of this sacrament and its pastoral focus. It is beyond the scope of this book to enter into the complex debate on this subject. The bibliographical materials found at the end of this book will direct the reader to some excellent resources for weighing the various arguments around conferring confirmation at particular ages. There cannot be a specifically "Hispanic" approach to confirmation developed apart from the wider context of the U.S. church. However, those who are rightly concerned that young people have an opportunity to affirm their faith and commitment to Christ and the church and who find the present discipline regarding confirmation theologically and pastorally troublesome may find the following discussion of the *Quince Años* celebration a way out of the impasse.

Quince Años

Belén was filled with mixed emotions. This was normal for a fifteen-year-old who was about to embark upon her *Quinceañera* year. Jesús was offering all the moral support he could, while Natividad was caught up in the dream that one day these feelings would also be hers. During these days, Carmen felt a special connection with her eldest daughter. Manuel became more quiet and more reflective as he wondered about Belén and the future that was opening up before her. Neither parent saw themselves

⚜

as being very traditional, in the sense that Belén had already been able to date unchaperoned a few times. On the other hand, they also felt apprehension and uncertainty as they watched their daughter take another step toward discovering her adult life. One day, sooner than they liked, she would step out on her own.

Carlos, the parish's permanent deacon, had made the Quince Años celebration one of his pastoral priorities. He not only wanted the celebration to be culturally appropriate but also wanted to ritualize the young people's rites of passage in faith and in life. In order to accomplish this, he had attended workshops where he gained good information about the celebration. He had listened to parents' stories of having to shop around in order to find a priest or deacon and a parish that would allow *la Quinceañera*. He had heard his pastor's and other priests' opinions about the excessive expense and superficial religiosity that went along with the birthday celebration. Carlos sought not a middle ground but rather a common ground where everyone could feel at home. He was more than an idealist, he was a dreamer. What follows is taken from Carlos's notes on Belén's Quince Años.

The parish plan had been worked on for a number of years. It was constantly being reevaluated and "fine-tuned."

1. The Quince Años was a parish event and was therefore celebrated at a parish Mass. Most people took the Saturday afternoon Mass.

2. The Quince Años was a family event and therefore the entire family was included in both the preparation and the celebration.

3. The Quince Años was a parish youth celebration, and therefore the youth ministry team helped to organize and run the retreat and prepare the Mass.

4. The Quince Años was for all young women and men who wanted to celebrate their fifteenth birthday in a special way.

CHAPTER 3

Three months before the Quince Años Mass, a meeting was set up with Carmen, Manuel and Belén. As was his custom, Father Kevin stopped in for a few minutes to greet everyone and to hear some of the responses to the questions. On this particular occasion, he noted how beautiful Carmen had grown with the years while he comically welcomed Manuel to the "old men's" club.

The questions were simple, to the point and directed to each member of the family: Why do you want to celebrate the Quince Años? What does it mean for you? How does this bring you closer to Jesus? Belén was told that she needed to write her own statement of faith to which she would commit herself. The Quince Años youth retreat would help her do this. Carmen and Manuel were asked to prepare a short statement as to why they were grateful to God for this moment. The retreat would also help them to orient their thoughts. The statements of faith and gratitude would be read at the Mass.

The youth ministry team planned a four-hour, Saturday-evening retreat for the young men and women of the parish who would be celebrating their Quince Años within the next couple of months. The novelty of having the young men also celebrate a Quince Años had not entirely worn off, but a tradition was gradually being built. Because things were done in groups and at Sunday Mass, more people had begun to take advantage of this event.

The retreat gathered the parents in one area where the teens related their tales about the trials and graces of their lives. Parents were to share their growing-up experiences in light of what they had heard. Afterward, they would write their statements of gratitude and share them with one another. The night would end in the church with a family reconciliation service which they could also celebrate in their homes.

The young people celebrating Quince Años gathered in another area to hear a short talk about the Hispanic culture. It was given

PAGE 74

by one of their peers who was born on this side of the *frontera* along with one who was born on the other side of the border. Next, they were divided into small groups and asked to answer three questions: What did they like about being a member of the Catholic church? What didn't they like? If they were God, how would they change the world? Carlos handled the group reports, stressing and affirming their insights. What made the usually exuberant group more quiet was the comment that they are the church, and if they like something, they should work to strengthen it, and if they don't like something, they are obligated to work for its change. "God changes the world through us, through them," he taught. The Quince Años young people were beginning to see that "when you grow up" was now. Decisions had to be made.

Belén became the example. She read the declaration of faith that she had been working on. She stood before a tribunal of her peers who asked if she really believed what she had spoken or simply repeated what her parents had told her. Her defense was sound and sure. She had made the decision to believe and act out her belief by joining the parish's AIDS support group. No further questions were needed. Each young person was asked to share their statement in a small group.

Father Kevin played his part well. He and Carlos knew their routine inside and out. They both recognized that the mention of the sacrament of reconciliation usually sent a cold chill down the spine of these Quince Años young people because of their mixed religious traditions. Some had been born in Mexico and Puerto Rico, where confession was usually prescribed before any communion. Others had learned that confession was not always necessary but without understanding why. Characteristic of their age, others were charting their own lives, which meant that they were rejecting the ways of their parents or any other person older than 25. Still others were just going through the motions by being in the confessional line. Father Kevin had had enough of his own heart-rending experiences with groups like this one to know that many of them, with tough and doubting faces, bore wounds of loneliness, isolation and alienation. His one-on-one confessional experiences were often tearful, even for some of the young men who finally found someone willing to listen and not judge. He found his own heart in them. He had nothing but admiration at how they disguised themselves behind the appearances of youthful superficiality.

The reconciliation routine was simple. Carlos played the part of different penitents, while Kevin played different confessor roles. Their antics and tactics usually produced rounds of laughter and an occasional applause of approval. With the precision of a professional comedy team, they began acting out the story of the prodigal son. The concluding question that haunted the now quiet and reflective audience was, "Where do you hurt?" Bridges between confessor and penitent were built; confidence between older and younger was established; the willingness to risk openness between two human beings was felt.

While individual confessions were happening with Father Kevin, Carlos was building another bridge of reconciliation. His task was to prepare the group for a concluding liturgy of the word with their parents. The Quince Años group and their parents would meet for a brief service of mutual forgiveness. Though not universally achieved, many reconnections were made that night.

The Mass

Father Kevin still squirmed at the sight of all the special dresses and suits that Belén, her attendants and her family wore. He wondered how Manuel and Carmen and the rest of the families, in spite of all their modernity, could lavish so much time and expense on celebrating such a ritual. His discomfort was eased by the warm welcome he received from the different young people who felt a connection with him. Carlos helped order the chaos of these opening moments.

With the liturgical resources at hand, Carlos developed a celebration adapted to the needs of the young people of San Martín Parish. The particularities of the Quince Años rite stressed the active participation of the young people present and their role in making the parish vibrant and strong. The actual rite began after the gospel and homily with Manuel and Carmen presenting their daughter to the parish community and giving voice to their prayer of gratitude. Belén, nervous yet resplendent, reaffirmed her baptismal vows in a clear, strong voice and then read her statement of belief. The various signs of commitment — ring, Bible, rosary, candle and the blessing by her parents — underlined her words.

What pleased Carlos most about this day was the secret that Belén had shared with him right before the ceremony began. She thanked him for all he had done to help her and her family get ready for this day. She also revealed her intention to become a part of the youth ministry team. Carlos knew she was a woman of her word.

Pastoral Notes

The exact origin of the Quince Años celebration is unknown. It probably stems from pre-Colombian rites of initiation for both boys and girls who were regarded as having "come of age" (and having become therefore marriageable). It was an example of what anthropologists call a "rite of passage" — a celebration that publicly acknowledges the changed social status of a member of a given society. For whatever reason, the tradition of initiating girls survived while a rite for the boys disappeared. In preparation for this rite, those girls turning 15 were separated from their childhood playmates and instructed in the wisdom of the community and in their duties as future wives and mothers. During the rite in its origins, the gods were thanked for the lives of these future mothers, and the young women pledged to fulfill their roles of service to the community. They were then honored with gifts, and a lavish fiesta took place. The Quinceañera was gradually Christianized by the missionaries to highlight a personal affirmation of faith by the young woman and her willingness to become a good Christian wife and mother. It then became common to celebrate it in the church, although apart from a Mass. Because of the rite's emphasis on the young woman's eligibility for marriage and her future role as a mother, young men traditionally participated in a secondary way as "escorts" but never as subjects of the rite. For this reason, in its more traditional form Quince Años often has all the trappings of a dress rehearsal for a wedding — complete with white dresses, bouquets, tuxedoed escorts and limousines. This "rite of passage" has a parallel in the Euro-American debutantes' ball or "coming out" celebration that usually takes place at a slightly later age.

Given the local Mexican origins of the celebration, it is not surprising that the Quinceañera is not consistently observed throughout Latin America. In the United States, however, it is becoming more common among non-Mexican Hispanic groups. Also, it is not uncommon for young people in the same family to have very different attitudes toward the celebration of Quince Años. Some young women enthusiastically enter into preparation for it and others choose not to take part in it at all.

In the previous discussion of the problem raised by confirmation, we saw that there has been growing dissatisfaction with the use of this sacrament as a rite of passage. This stems from familiarity with the renewed theology of initiation presented in the RCIA and from the recovery of the traditional order of celebrating the sacraments of initiation: first baptism, then confirmation, then eucharist. It is especially problematic from a theological point of view to use confirmation as an adolescent rite of Christian maturity, since the sacrament originated in the West as the bishop's intervention in the process of initiation.

In the United States and elsewhere in the Hispanic world, Quinceañeras also have become problematic. Pastors in some parts of the country, and even pastors who are very sympathetic to preserving Hispanic customs, find it difficult to deal with what is perceived to be the exaggerated expense and superficiality that sometimes accompany this celebration. The poor often do not have Quiceañeras, simply because they are too expensive. In addition to this objection is the fact that it seems anachronistic, at least in this country. A young woman is no longer considered ready for marriage at 15 in the late-twentieth-century United States, regardless of her ethnic background. What are we also saying about the respective social and ecclesial roles of men and women if it is only young women who pledge to live their faith, while there is no corresponding rite for young men?

For these reasons, there has been a move in many parts of the country to rethink both the age of confirmation and the practice of Quinceañera. Happily, it seems that a Quince Años celebration may be a pastoral solution to the problematic age of confirmation. If confirmation is celebrated at the time of first communion, when the child is in the second or third grade (the age recommended by tradition and canon law; see canon 891), a Quince Años celebration then naturally fills the need for a liturgical rite for adolescents, those in or near the eighth grade. Therefore, this rite needs to be opened up to young men as well as to young women; hence the shift in terminology from *Quinceañera* to *Quince Años*. This celebration, then, can serve as the focal point for youth ministry by creating a powerful ritual in which the support of both parents and parish community encourages them to pledge their faith in Christ and the church publicly as they approach the threshold of young adulthood.

While this may seem to be a controversial proposal, it clearly answers the need for a more effective outreach to adolescents, especially second-generation Hispanic adolescents, who have to deal with a perplexing array of issues at this stage in their lives. Questions of cultural identity that often lead to alienation and isolation, tensions caused by poverty, discrimination, gangs, drugs and widespread teenage pregnancy all affect the life of Hispanic youth in this country. Rather than refusing to offer Quince Años celebrations on the grounds that they are anachronistic and inappropriately expensive, parishes can use the celebration as a "teachable moment" and provide a forum for young people to choose that which is life-giving and positive. The moment also underlines the importance of family and parish community in supporting its young people at this crucial time in their lives.

Clearly, this celebration should be seen as the culmination of a period of preparation. This is why, in the preceding vignette, the description of the Quince Años retreat figured so prominently. Locating the Quince Años celebration in a weekend Mass — celebrated for individuals or groups of young people and with the entire parish community present — serves to strengthen the communal aspect of the rite. It also plays down the need for each family to spend a lavish amount on the celebration. The rite found in this chapter is very simple and could be adapted to local custom. One important aspect to the rite, however, is inviting the participation of all those present in the various aspects of the celebration. The Quince Años young people should be asked and then trained to serve in various liturgical roles — lectoring, greeting, preparing the altar table and serving as ministers of communion.

Quince Años and Reconciliation

The celebration of the sacrament of reconciliation among Hispanic young people can be a humbling experience for both confessor and penitent. These young people, like the rest of the church, struggle with the meaning of this moment. They are often confused by their parents' understanding of confession, since it is still often conditioned by a certain pre–Vatican II catechesis as well as by cultural tendencies that are in strong contrast with their own catechetical formation. Despite these problems, the Quince Años retreat is a prime catechetical opportunity for Hispanic young people to experience the important role this sacrament can play in Christian life.

The practice of confession within the Hispanic community is very diverse. Many consider normative what they were taught in their countries of origin. For families from rural backgrounds, the priest came once a year on the patronal feast day. Confession became a requirement for anyone taking advantage of his presence by having their children baptized, celebrating first confession and first communion, having marriages validated and having the sick anointed. In urban settings in Latin America it is not unusual for confessions to be heard right before Sunday Mass or — although against the spirit of the liturgy — during the celebration of Mass in some situations. For Hispanics born and catechized in the United States, the Vatican II structure, style and practice influence the meaning of "regular confessions" and how sin is perceived.

It is both interesting and confusing to note that the sacrament is referred to as reconciliation while the rite is termed penance, and all the while people still call it confession. Each word — reconciliation, penance, confession — bears a particular grace and burden, depicts a particular attitude and symbolizes the way the sacrament is approached. Generally speaking, the Hispanic community still refers to the sacrament of confession. It is a private moment to "come clean" before God through naming one's personal sins and receiving absolution from the priest. The phrase *me acuso, padre* (I accuse myself, Father) introduces the penitent's listing of sins and serves as a key phrase which sums up the meaning of "confession" for many Hispanics.

Crossing the border into the U.S. religious experience of confession nuances the Hispanic attitude even further. Through their sacramental preparation programs, children receive a catechesis that highlights the reconciliation aspect of the sacrament. In acknowledging our sin and imperfection, we can always rely on God's grace and mercy. The emphasis in this catechesis is on God's gracious, generous and loving forgiveness. Communal celebrations of reconciliation underline the communitarian characteristic of this liturgical experience. Though different from the catechetical instruction of their grandparents and parents, this renewed emphasis on reconciliation does not do away with the more traditional understanding of the sacrament but complements it.

Sin and forgiveness within the Hispanic community are not seen in the abstract but are seen as a relationship. Missing Mass on Sunday is sinful not primarily because one violates an abstract law but because it indirectly shows a lack of respect to those who have taught you: parents, godparents, priests, catechists. Sinfulness and culpability are experienced differently by men and women. Hispanic women confess the sins of their family. They feel responsible if their son/daughter lives with a partner before marriage. Family arguments, the husband's reluctance to come to Mass and their own personal offenses are intertwined in their confessions. Their sense of sin is communal, and so their confession is frequent. Forgiveness is a sharing of an unbearable burden, an insoluble dilemma. It is the woman who teaches the spiritual life to her family by example. Men tend to see church rules, obligations and requirements as ideals to be strived toward rather than as absolute norms. The ideas represent a goal that we hope to reach one day, but until that day arrives, failure is part of the human condition. Sinfulness is something all humans share. Forgiveness acknowledges dependence on another.

Confession, for Hispanic men and women, is seen as a preparation rite for other sacramental moments when they would be expected to receive communion. There are other natural *tiempos fuertes* (important times) that are confessional occasions: patronal feasts, novenas in honor of Nuestra Señora de Guadalupe, retreats, *cursillos*, missions, Lent and Holy Week. These events call a person to confession in order to "properly" prepare for and enter into the celebration.

Within this context, an invitation to receive the sacrament of reconciliation during a Quince Años retreat is also an evangelical opportunity to seed the fertile hearts of Hispanic young people with the good seed of the word. The long-term hope is that a harvest of Christ's mercy will be reaped in their adult lives when they remember this retreat. It is extremely important that they find in their confessor a good listener and a compassionate friend.

Misa para los Quince Años

MONICIÓN POR UNO DE LOS PADRES
DESPUÉS DEL EVANGELIO

En este día tan especial, queremos a dar gracias a Dios por tantas cosas bonitas que hemos vivido en este sueño que lleva ya quince años.

En esta eucaristía queremos proclamar: gracias, Señor Dios, por habernos dado hijos e hijas como N. y N. Les amamos como Tú les amas, desde antes de que nacieran.

Su presentación a la asamblea de la Iglesia hoy, es para nosotros tan importante como la de su bautismo, porque están pasando por una edad muy importante en su vida. Hoy nuevamente queremos consagrarles a Dios, entregarles a El.

Con la familia de Dios aquí reunida te pedimos que siempre le lleves de su mano y le libres de todos los peligros. Que El les conceda realizar sus más hermosos sueños y ser muy felices.

Homilia

RENOVACIÓN DE LAS PROMESAS BAUTISMALES POR LOS JÓVENES QUE CELEBRAN SUS QUINCE AÑOS

Mientras están de pie entre el pueblo, los jóvenes renuevan sus promesas bautismales como una expresión de su fidelidad y compromiso a Cristo y a su Iglesia.

Celebrante: Reciban la luz de Cristo. En el día de su bautismo, sus padres y padrinos hablaron en sus nombres. Ahora, tomen esta luz y proclamen por ustedes mismos su fe en Cristo.

Cada joven prende una vela del cirio pascual.

A Quince Años Eucharistic Celebration

INTRODUCTION MADE BY ONE OF THE PARENTS
AFTER THE GOSPEL

On this special day, we parents thank God for so many wonderful things that we have experienced throughout the past fifteen years.

In this eucharist we say: Thank you, Lord, for having given us sons and daughters like N. and N. We have loved them like you, Lord, love them — even before they were born.

Like their baptism, their presentation to our parish family today is very important because it signals that they have come to an important turning point in their lives. As we did at their baptism, we, again, want to consecrate and commend them to God.

In the presence of this assembly, we ask that they always be held in God's loving hand and that they be protected from all danger. We pray for their happiness and that God grant that their most beautiful dreams become a reality.

Homily

RENEWAL OF BAPTISMAL PROMISES BY THOSE
CELEBRATING THEIR QUINCE AÑOS

Standing in the midst of the assembly, the young people renew their baptismal commitment. In doing so they express their fidelity and commitment to Christ and to the church.

Presider: Receive the light of Christ. On the day of your baptism, your parents and godparents spoke in your name. Now, take this light and proclaim your faith in Christ.

Each young person lights a candle from the paschal candle.

Celebrante:
Hermanos y hermanas:
Por el Misterio Pascual
hemos sido sepultados con Cristo en el bautismo,
para que vivamos una vida nueva.
Renovemos las promesas del santo bautismo
con las que en otro tiempo renunciamos a Satanás
y sus obras, y prometimos servir fielmente
a Dios en la santa Iglesia católica.
Así pues:
¿Renuncian a Satanás, es decir:
— al pecado, como negación de Dios
— al mal, como consecuencia del pecado
— a la violencia, como opuesta a la caridad?
R: Sí, renuncio.

Celebrante: ¿Renuncian a sus obras, es decir:
— a buscar solamente las satisfacciones corporales
   y los deleites de los sentidos
— a la injusticia y discriminación
— a la falta de fe y de confianza en Dios?
R: Sí, renuncio.

Celebrante: ¿Renuncian a sus seducciones, es decir:
— a encerrarles en su egoísmo
— a considerarles superiores a los demás
— a creerles convertidos definitivamente?
R: Sí, renuncio.

Celebrante: ¿Creen en Dios, Padre todopoderoso,
   creador del cielo y de la tierra?
R: Sí creo.

Presider:

Dear friends,

through the paschal mystery

we were buried with Christ in baptism

so that we may rise with him to a new life.

Renew the promises you made at baptism

when you rejected Satan and his works,

and promised to serve God faithfully

in the holy Catholic church.

And so:

Do you reject Satan whose presence is apparent in:

— sin as a rejection of God

— evil, as a consequence of sin

— and in violence, as the opposite of love?

R: I do.

Presider: Do you reject his works, such as

— a selfish obsession with bodily pleasure

— injustice and discrimination of any kind

— and a lack of faith and confidence in God?

R: I do.

Presider: Do you reject his seductions, such as

— closing yourself off from others

— considering yourself better than your neighbor

— and believing yourself in no further need of conversion

R: I do.

Presider: Do you believe in God, the Father almighty,

  creator of heaven and earth?

R: I do.

Celebrante: ¿Creen en Jesucristo, su único Hijo, nuestro Señor, que nació de santa María Virgen, murió, fue sepultado, resucitó de entre los muertos y está sentado a la derecha del Padre?
R: Sí creo.

Celebrante: ¿Creen en el Espíritu Santo, en la santa Iglesia católica, en la comunión de los santos, en el perdón de los pecados, en la resurrección de los muertos y en la vida eterna?
R: Sí creo.

Celebrante: Que Dios todopoderoso, Padre de nuestro Señor Jesucristo, que les regeneró por el agua y el Espíritu Santo y les concedió la remisión de los pecados, les guarde en su gracia, en el mismo Jesucristo nuestro Señor, para la vida eterna.
R: Amén.

DECLARACIÓN PERSONAL DE LOS QUINCE AÑOS

BENDICIÓN DE LOS PADRES

Los padres están invitados a acercarse para bendecir a sus hijos en su manera tradicional.

Celebrante: Queridos jóvenes, en el nombre de toda la Iglesia aquí presente en esta asamblea, recibo su compromiso con alegría de seguir a Cristo y servir a su pueblo. Y que Dios, que empezó tan buen trabajo en ustedes, lo concluya en el Día de Cristo Jesús.

La asamblea se afirma el compromiso en una manera apropiada.

Presider: Do you believe in Jesus Christ,
   his only Son, our Lord,
who was born of the Virgin Mary,
was crucified, died, and was buried,
rose from the dead,
and is now seated at the right hand of the Father?
R: I do.

Presider: Do you believe in the Holy Spirit,
the holy Catholic church, the communion of saints,
the forgiveness of sins, the resurrection of the body,
and life everlasting?
R: I do.

Presider: God, the all powerful Father of our Lord Jesus Christ,
has given you a new birth by water and the Holy Spirit
and forgiveness of all your sins.
May he also keep you faithful to our Lord Jesus Christ
for ever and ever.
R: Amen.

PERSONAL STATEMENT BY EACH
QUINCE AÑOS YOUNG PERSON

BLESSING BY THE PARENTS

The parents are now invited to come forward to bless their children in their traditional manner.
   Presider: Dear friends, in the name of the church here
   present in this assembly, I joyfully receive your commitment
   to follow Christ and to serve his people. And may God who
   has begun this good work in you, bring it to completion on the
   Day of Christ Jesus.
The assembly acknowledges the commitment in an appropriate way.

Questions for Reflection

1. From the church's perspective, what are the graces and tempta-tions that young people from this community find supportive or confrontational?

2. From the parents' perspective, what are the hopes and fears they have for their children in this parish community? How can the parish help them strengthen these hopes and challenge these fears?

3. From the young people's perspective, where do they find life and support in this community? Where do they confront death? In what way is their faith a source of life, hope or strength for them?

4. What are the identifying characteristics of Hispanic young people's spirituality? How can these be affirmed publicly at our Sunday liturgy?

5. Who are the unofficial "peer" ministers in this parish community?

6. What are the local "rites of initiation" into adulthood that are already taking place? Do these need to be supported or challenged?

Rites of Betrothal and Marriage

Pedir la Mano

he midnight long-distance phone call awakened Marcos, Jesús's childhood friend. As he rubbed his face into consciousness, Marcos became aware of the anxious tone in Jesús's voice even before he comprehended the words themselves. Marcos asked his *carnal* (good friend) to calm down and repeat what he had just said. "Tomorrow night my parents and I are going to *pedir la mano de Anita*. We're going to talk to her parents about getting married. I'm nervous as hell because I think they may say no. Can you give me any advice?" Jesús's request struck Marcos so spontaneously that all he could do was laugh and laugh uncontrollably. "What are you laughing about?" shouted Jesús, half hurt, half angry at his friend's unexpected response. In a tone of voice that bridged the gap between them, Marcos simply said, "For this you wake me up at midnight? This is just the beginning of what it means to be married. You're never going to know the answer any better, so get ready. This is great. Call me tomorrow night after it's all over and let me know what happens."

The involvement of Anita's parents in this aspect of the relationship, the *pedir la mano*, is important. It signals the support of family and community that Jesús and Anita, indeed all couples, will need to make the commitment to spend the rest of their lives together. Jesús's friend Marcos could sense the anxiety in his friend because this ritual at the beginning of the marriage process means such a great deal. How Anita's parents would respond to his expression of his intentions would be a crucial moment.

Manuel and Carmen's oldest child, Jesús, met Anita in the parish adult confirmation class. Besides liking the way she looked, he liked what she had to say. She asked straightforward questions and wasn't afraid to say that she disagreed. He even liked the way she refused his first invitations to go out with him. By chance they were assigned to the same confirmation discussion group and, according to Father Kevin, through the work of the Holy Spirit they came to know, like and love one another.

Over time Anita and Jesús came to appreciate the uniqueness in their meeting within the context of the adult confirmation class. Their renewed interest in Christianity and in celebrating the sacrament of confirmation as adults gave them a common foundation as well as content for their initial conversations when getting to know one another. It increased their interest in one another and in their hope that the relationship would continue to grow strong.

Anita was the oldest of eight brothers and sisters, half of whom were born in the United States and half of whom were citizens of Mexico. Anita was born on the border, within the United States, but raised in Ciudad Juárez, Mexico. Like Jesús, it was her decision to

delay confirmation, and it was her decision to finally receive it. It was also her decision to follow the "rules" of getting married according to Mexican customs. The first step was the tradition of *pedir la mano,* when the parents of the would-be groom and the parish priest meet with the young woman's parents. In this dialogue, Manuel and Carmen, Jesús's parents, ask Anita's parents for their permission for the marriage of Jesús and Anita.

The parishioners of San Martín de Porres parish had grown accustomed to having engaged couples announce their upcoming wedding during the Sunday Mass. The involvement of the community of faith in the traditional rites leading up to the marriage rite iself further the support of family and friends.

Extending the *pedir la mano* to the public announcement of the coming marriage lessens the separation of pastoral rites — like weddings and funerals — from the regular assembly at the table of the Lord for Sunday eucharist. Such separations can keep the community of faith removed from the rites of passage through which all human beings must move, and these separations can also miss opportunities to bring back to the faith family members who have fallen away and have had little contact with the liturgy in years.

During the dismissal rite, Carlos, the deacon, would invite by name those who were entering into the marriage preparation program. The engaged couples and their parents would then come forward. After voicing their intention to be married, each couple would turn to their parents and ask for their blessing. Then Father Kevin and the entire assembly would extend their hands over the couples as a special blessing was proclaimed. This would be followed by congratulatory applause.

La Boda

The wedding day arrived all too quickly. Marcos was there as the *chambelán de honor* (best man). Anita had chosen her youngest sister Juana as the *dama de honor* (maid of honor). The *padrinos de velación* (official witnesses) were Carlos and his wife, Cristina. In addition to these couples, Kevin concentrated on the other "church" *padrinos: cojines* (cushions), *anillos* (rings), *libro y rosario* (prayerbook and rosary), *lazo* (wedding cord), *arras* (wedding coins), *el ramo de la Virgen* (bouquet for Mary's altar) and the *pajes* (literally the wedding "pages": ring bearer, flower girl, and children to carry the bride's veil in procession). These seven pairs of women and men and children formed the nucleus of the wedding ceremony. The other 20 or so couples, *padrinos, madrinas, damas y chambelanes* would perform their role at the wedding reception.

After having witnessed so many marriages, Father Kevin had developed a way to effectively include these Hispanic elements in a simple wedding rite. The *cojines* were placed on the kneelers of the bride and groom by the corresponding *padrinos* during the entrance procession. After the homily, the customary statement of intentions and exchange of vows took place. After this came the blessing and exchange of rings. The blessing of the *arras* (the wedding coins) was adapted recently in order to reflect the husband and wife's shared responsibility of providing for the economic and material welfare of the home. It was further modified to express the couple's concern for the poor. The *libro* and *rosario* were blessed and received with words that signified the couple's desire to form their marriage around prayer and devotion to Mary. The *lazo,* or cord, without words was draped around the couple during the singing of the *Holy, Holy,* and later removed after the nuptial blessing.

During the nuptial blessing, the parents of both the bride and groom were asked to stand next to Father Kevin in order to extend their hands over their children. In a way reminiscent of their engagement ceremony, and instead of asking for their parents' blessing before leaving for the church, Jesús and Anita publicly asked their parents for the traditional blessing, which was duly imparted with tears and embraces. After communion, Kevin invited the newlyweds to offer a prayer at Mary's altar for themselves and for all who had brought them to this day. Led by Marcos and Juana, Anita placed the *ramo de la Virgen* on the altar as Jesús placed incense on burning coals in a censer prepared in front of the shrine.

Marcos, both nervous and happy while watching the ceremony unfold, remembered the midnight phone call and laughed silently to himself.

Pastoral Notes

The Hispanic community is both in touch and in tension with their particular rites that interpret the celebration of the sacraments. This ought not to be seen as problematic but rather as a creative opportunity for evangelization and encounter with the death and rising of Christ reflected in these traditions. The perdurance of special customs used in the celebration of the sacraments among Hispanics, especially those from Mexico and Puerto Rico, is due largely to the fact that they return home not only for family visits but also for baptisms, marriages and funerals. Because of this continuing contact, they maintain an acquaintance with these traditional rites and expect that they will be used in the celebration of the sacraments back in the United States. The tension arises precisely in adapting these customs to the new cultural situation in which Hispanics find themselves in this country. This is especially true for Latinos of the second generation born in the United States.

A good example of the confusion that can sometimes arise due to the different marriage customs is in identifying the official witnesses for the marriage. The *padrinos de velación* (or *de la iglesia*) customarily are married and sit next to the bride and groom. They are the official witnesses. In the United States it is the best man and maid (or matron) of honor (the *chambelán* and *dama de honor*) who fulfill this official role. A pastoral headache can be prevented if, in consultation with the *novios,* the *padrinos* kneel with them, thus being the official witnesses, while the *chambelán* and *dama de honor* accompany the newlyweds to Mary's altar, thus giving them special recognition. In order to please their parents, the *novios* will need to reflect on the wedding customs that will be followed and how these traditions need to be adapted. The important thing is that there be an openness to celebrating these rites. When the rites are enriched with an appropriate prayer text and highlighted during the celebration, usually everyone is well pleased.

The rites of betrothal and marriage described in the preceding vignette are adapted into an ideal setting: All involved are conscious of their traditions. Depending upon their degree of cultural assimilation, some young Hispanic couples may be unfamiliar with many of these practices, or at least unaware of their significance.

There are no specific church rites for engagement. What we have done here is connect what often happens privately in the family with the larger parish family through an engagement ceremony. The rite, following traditional Hispanic practice, emphasizes that a pledge to marry involves more than the couple but also affects the immediate family of the future bride and groom as well as the larger community. By making this pledge, the engaged couple enters into what anthropologists and others call a *liminal* state (from the Latin word *limen,* threshold.) Their status in relation to their family and society is in the process of changing. They are no longer really single, nor are they married. This

period of betrothal is meant to serve as a time of transition and preparation. It is often the case that the parish or diocese requires the couple
to attend some kind of program in order to help the *novios* reflect on
their decision to marry and the role that their faith will play in their
marriage. It thus seems appropriate to affirm and confirm the tentative
commitment made by the couple within the greater family that is the
local church by means of a simple blessing at the end of a Sunday Mass.

   As with the other rites of passage we have seen so far (baptism, first communion, Quince Años), the wedding rite not only involves
the immediate family but many of the couple's extended relationships
as well. Thus, Hispanic wedding parties tend to be large. *Padrinos* and
madrinas are usually married friends who help pay for the expenses of
the marriage. The *padrinos de velación/iglesia* pay the stole fee to the
priest and serve as the official witnesses, while other church-related
padrinos pay for the rings, *arras, cojines, libro y rosario* and *ramo de la
Virgen*. The "wedding feast" *padrinos* (of whom there may be several
couples) join together and underwrite the cost of the reception: the wedding meal, liquor, cake, musicians, and so on. The *damas* and *chambelanes* form a "wedding court." They are often chosen from among family
members who are single (brothers, sisters, cousins) and friends. The
church *padrinos* are of most importance during the actual wedding.
They need to sit in the front pews in order to carry out their duties. All
others are included in the entrance and dismissal processions.

   Including the *cojines* and *anillos* in the wedding rite is not
particularly difficult. The *cojines* are placed on the kneelers of the bride
and groom by the designated *padrinos* during the entrance procession.
Thus, the *padrinos de los cojines* should be the first couple in the bridal
procession. The exchange of rings occurs in much the same way as it
is usually done in the United States.

The *arras* have a long and venerable history. Interestingly, the word *arras* comes from the Greek word *arrabon,* which means "pledge," and originally referred to the giving of "earnest money," or dowry. In parts of the Latin West, the actual exchange of vows borrowed this term and was called the *ordo arrarum,* or "the rite of pledges," and coins sealed the pledge. Over time, twelve or even thirteen coins (a "baker's dozen," signifying prosperity) were given by the husband to the wife to seal the "contract" of marriage and to show that he was economically capable of supporting his wife and a family. The rite we present below, while retaining the use of the *arras* is adapted to reflect a new social situation and a renewed understanding of the sacrament of marriage as a mutual covenant. The traditional words that accompany the groom giving the *arras* to the bride emphasized the husband's role in relation to the wife. Since most couples' economic survival now depends on two incomes, wives equally share in the economic support of the family. This reality must be acknowledged. We are also proposing another formula for the *arras* in order to accentuate the meaning of the marriage as a sacrament of service to the larger community — a way of living out the gospel. The new formula reflects the sentiment found in one of the petitions of the first form of the final blessing: that the couple be such witnesses of God's love in the world to the poor and afflicted, that the bride and groom will be welcomed into the kingdom of heaven by those whom they have helped.

There are no customary words for the blessing and giving of the *libro, rosario* and *lazo.* Simple words highlighting the meaning of prayer, scripture and Marian devotions are certainly appropriate and are suggested below. Traditionally, the *libro* (a hand missal) and rosary were presented to the bride as a sign of her duty to pray for the family. Rather than giving the impression that prayer is the exclusive duty of the wife, we suggest that these be presented to the couple. In lieu of a hand missal, which is no longer necessary for full participation in the eucharist, we suggest substituting a Bible.

The *lazo,* a ribbon, cord or double rosary, binds the bride and groom together. Without a blessing or words, we have placed this ritual after the singing of the Holy, Holy. Then, as the *novios* kneel for the eucharistic prayer, the *padrinos* place the *lazo* over the shoulders of the bride and groom. Sometimes the bride's veil is also draped over the shoulder of the groom in silence. The *lazo* remains in place up to the nuptial blessing, after which it is removed in order to leave the couple free to offer the sign of peace.

The nuptial blessing includes the parents (or their substitutes), who are invited to bless their children with the presider. At the time of the blessing (after the Lord's Prayer) the *novios'* parents are asked to stand with the presider and extend their hands over their children in a gesture of blessing. Three forms of the nuptial blessing are given in the rite. We have provided the third form below. Once again, the emphasis here is placed on the family context of the rites and acknowledges the union of two families through marriage.

The offering of flowers at the Marian shrine after communion is expanded to include the groom. Since the marriage rite itself speaks of the two becoming one during the exchange of vows, it seems appropriate that they should not be separated ritually after this moment. The bride's traditional solo visit to Mary's altar could convey the wrong message — that prayer and devotion is women's work and not something appropriately engaged in by men. Therefore, we are suggesting that the groom accompany the bride to the Marian shrine and offer incense while she offers the flowers. In this way, their common prayer may be presented to God through Mary's intercession. We also suggest that the *chambelán* and the *dama de honor* accompany the couple — not only to assist with the bride's train but to ritually highlight the fact that, as close friends or family, they will be walking in faith with the couple.

A sign that Hispanic lives and liturgy are not sealed off from the influence of U.S. culture is the growing wish to use the new U.S. custom of the so-called "unity candle." This large candle, usually decorated with a Chi Rho and two conjoined rings symbolizing Christian marriage, is solemnly lit by the bride and groom from two smaller candles that are then extinguished. It usually takes place at the end of the marriage rite and just prior to the prayers of intercession. In some ways its inclusion in a Hispanic wedding represents an intrusion into what is already a rather complex series of nuptial symbols. This custom originated in the Euro-American church, whose interpretation of the marriage rite has been rightly criticized as being symbolically impoverished and overly cerebral. Commentators have also criticized this rite as unintentionally conveying a wrong idea about marriage — especially when the two smaller candles are extinguished. This ritual act could be interpreted as the couples losing their individual identities in the context of marriage. Pastoral practice will need to reflect on adding this rite to a Hispanic marriage already replete with traditional symbols.

Finally, pastoral ministers should be aware that, because of the different ways marriage is civilly regulated in Latin American countries, misunderstandings can arise. For example, in Mexico, where a marriage witnessed by a church minister is not recognized by the government, the couple is first married civilly by a magistrate. Later they arrange for marriage in the church. Therefore, it sometimes happens that a couple (especially from Mexico) will have their marriage witnessed by a justice of the peace and then come to church for the nuptial Mass. When the priest or deacon asks for the wedding license and finds that it has already been filed because they were married civilly, he needs to be sensitive rather than condemnatory. On the other hand, couples from other Latin American countries that have concordats with the Holy See will sometimes be under the impression that the church wedding completely takes care of all of the civil requirements for marriage. Under the old concordat in Colombia, for example, to be married civilly, the couple had to go to the chancery office and abjure the Catholic faith. In light of this diversity, it is important to ask the couple about their understanding of the legal requirements involved with marriage in order to avoid last-minute misunderstandings.

Celebración del Matrimonio dentro de la Misa

Rito de Entrada

Liturgia de la Palabra

Homilía

Procúrese un momento de silencio y reflexión después de la homilía.
Todos se ponen de pie. Sería conveniente que los esposos estuvieran
colocados de tal modo que no diesen la espalda a la asamblea.

Rito del Matrimonio

Celebrante:

Han venido aquí, hermanos, para que el Señor, ante el ministro
de la Iglesia y ante esta comunidad cristiana, consagre con
su sello el amor que ustedes se tienen.

Este amor Cristo lo bendice abundantemente, y con
un nuevo sacramento, a ustedes, a quienes por el bautismo ya
ha santificado, los va a enriquecer y a dar fuerza para que se
guarden siempre mutua fidelidad y puedan cumplir las demás
obligaciones del matrimonio.

Así pues, ante esta comunidad cristiana que representa
a la Iglesia, les pregunto:

N. y N., ¿han venido aquí a contraer matrimonio por
su libre y plena voluntad y sin que nada ni nadie los presione?

¿Están dispuestos a amarse y honrarse mutuamente
durante toda la vida?

La siguiente pregunta puede omitirse, si las circunstancias lo aconsejan,
por ejemplo, si los contrayentes son de edad avanzada.

¿Están dispuestos a recibir con amor los hijos que Dios le dé,
y a educarlos según la ley de Cristo y de su Iglesia?

Rite for Celebrating Marriage during Mass

ENTRANCE RITE

LITURGY OF THE WORD

Homily

Be sure to allow a time of silence and reflection after the homily. All then stand. It would be appropriate for the couple to be positioned in such a way that they do not show their backs to the assembly.

RITE OF MARRIAGE

Presider:

My dear friends, you have come together in this church so that the Lord may seal and strengthen your love in the presence of the church's minister and this community.

Christ abundantly blesses this love. He has already consecrated you in baptism, and now he enriches and strengthens you by a special sacrament so that you may assume the duties of marriage in mutual and lasting fidelity.

And so, in the presence of the church, I ask you to state your intentions.

N. and N., have you come here freely and without reservation to give yourselves to each other in marriage?

Will you love and honor each other as husband and wife for the rest of your lives?

The following question may be omitted if, for example, the couple is advanced in years.

Will you accept children lovingly from God, and bring them up according to the law of Christ and his church?

Consentimiento

Celebrante: Así pues, ya que quieren establecer entre ustedes la alianza santa del matrimonio, unan sus manos y expresen su consentimiento delante de Dios y de su Iglesia.

El novio dice:
Yo, N., te acepto a ti, N., como mi esposa y prometo serte fiel en lo próspero y en lo adverso, en la salud y en la enfermedad, y amarte y respetarte todos los días de mi vida.

La novia dice:
Yo, N., te acepto a ti, N., como mi esposo y prometo serte fiel en lo próspero y en lo adverso, en la salud y en la enfermedad, y amarte y respetarte todos los días de mi vida.

Celebrante:
Que el Señor confirme este consentimiento que han manifestado ante la Iglesia, y cumpla en ustedes su bendición. Lo que Dios acaba de unir, no lo separe el hombre.
R: Amén.

Se puede usar agua bendita para bendecir las manos de los novios.

Aclamación de la Asamblea

El celebrante, a continuación, puede invitar a la asamblea con estas palabras u otras semejantes:
Proclamemos la bondad de Dios para con estos dos hijos suyos.

La asamblea responde:
Bendito sea Dios, que los ha unido. Aleluya, aleluya.

También un solista puede cantar o proclamar la aclamación, que después repite la asamblea.

CONSENT

Since it is your intention to enter into marriage, join your right hands, and declare your consent before God and his church.

The bridegroom says:
I, N., take you, N., to be my wife. I promise to be true to you in good times and in bad, in sickness and in health. I will love you and honor you all the days of my life.

The bride says:
I, N., take you, N., to be my husband. I promise to be true to you in good times and in bad, in sickness and in health. I will love you and honor you all the days of my life.

Presider:
You have declared your consent before the church. May the Lord in his goodness strengthen your consent and fill you both with his blessings.
What God has joined, no one must divide.
R: Amen.

Holy water may be used to bless the hands of the newlyweds.

ACCLAMATION OF THE ASSEMBLY

The presider may then say:
Let us proclaim how good God has been toward this couple.

The assembly responds:
Blessed be God who has made them one. Alleluia, alleluia.

A soloist may sing or proclaim the acclamation that is then repeated by the assembly.

BENDICIÓN DE LOS ANILLOS Y DE LAS ARRAS CON AGUA BENDITA

Celebrante:
Bendice + Señor, a estos hijos tuyos, N. y N.,
y santifícalos en tu amor,
y que estos anillos y estas arras,
símbolo de fidelidad y de ayuda mutua,
las recuerden siempre
el cariño que se tienen.
Por nuestro Señor Jesucristo. Amen.

ENTREGA DE LOS ANILLOS

El esposo coloca en el dedo anular de su esposa el anillo destinado a ella, diciendo, si es oportuno:
N., recibe este anillo
como signo de mi amor y de mi fidelidad.
En el nombre del Padre y del Hijo
y del Espíritu Santo.

De la misma manera, la esposa coloca el anillo destinado a su esposo en el dedo anular de éste, diciendo, si es oportuno:
N., recibe este anillo
como signo de mi amor y de mi fidelidad.
En el nombre del Padre y del Hijo
y del Espíritu Santo.

ENTREGA DE LAS ARRAS

Luego, el esposo toma las arras y, teniéndolas entre las manos juntas, las entrega a la esposa que las recibe con las dos manos debajo de las de su esposo.
El esposo:
N., estas arras representan el fruto de nuestra labor.
Recíbelas como signo del esfuerzo nuestro

BLESSING OF THE RINGS AND *ARRAS* WITH HOLY WATER

Presider:

Lord, bless + and consecrate N. and N.
in their love for one another,
and may these rings and these *arras,*
symbols of faithfulness and mutual support,
be constant reminders of the
love they have for each other.
We ask this through Christ our Lord. Amen.

EXCHANGE OF RINGS

The bridegroom places his wife's ring on her ring finger.
He may say:

N., take this ring
as a sign of my love and fidelity.
In the name of the Father, and of the Son,
    and of the Holy Spirit.

The bride places her husband's ring on his ring finger.
She may say:

N., take this ring
as a sign of my love and fidelity.
In the name of the Father, and of the Son,
    and of the Holy Spirit.

BESTOWAL OF THE *ARRAS*

Then the bridegroom takes the arras, and holding them with two hands,
lets them fall into the cupped hands of his wife, who has placed her hands
below those of her husband.

The bridegroom:

N., these *arras* represent the fruit of our labor.
Receive them as a sign of our striving

de vivir una vida sencilla
siguiendo a Cristo y a su Evangelio.

La esposa:
N., las recibo en señal del cuidado que tendremos y
de compartir nuestros bienes con los más necesitados
que encontramos en el camino de la vida.

ENTREGA DEL LIBRO Y DEL ROSARIO

El celebrante entrega la Biblia y el rosario a la pareja, diciendo:
Reciban este libro que tiene la Palabra de Dios;
reciban también este rosario
para que su hogar sea un lugar de oración,
un lugar que se hace santo
por la confianza y el amor que tienen en
las promesas del Salvador
y en la intercesión de
su madre, María, la Virgen Santísima.

ORACIÓN DE LOS FIELES

LITURGIA EUCARÍSTICA

Oración sobre las ofrendas
Prefacio
Santo, Santo, Santo
Después de haber cantado el Santo, los padrinos del lazo colocan el lazo
sobre los hombros de la pareja en silencio.
Plegaria Eucarística
Padre Nuestro

to live a simple life
as disciples of Christ and his gospel.

The bride:
N., I accept these *arras* as a sign of the
concern that we will have during our married life
in sharing our goods with those in need.

GIVING OF THE BIBLE AND ROSARY

The presider gives the Bible and the rosary to the newlyweds saying:
Receive this book of God's Word;
receive also this rosary.
May your home be a place of prayer —
a place made holy by the confidence and love
that you have in the promises of Christ
and in the intercession of his mother, Mary,
the Blessed Virgin. Amen.

PRAYER OF THE FAITHFUL

LITURGY OF THE EUCHARIST

Prayer over the Gifts
Preface
Holy, Holy, Holy
After the Holy, Holy is sung, the padrinos del lazo place the cord or large
rosary on the shoulders of the couple in silence.
Eucharistic Prayer
Our Father

❧❧

Bendición Nupcial por la Esposa y el Esposo

Después del Padre Nuestro se omite el Líbranos Señor, y se invita a los padres de la esposa y del esposo a venir al lado del celebrante.

Vuelto hacia los contrayentes, con las manos juntas, el celebrante invita a todos a orar, diciendo:

Hermanos y hermanas, pidámosle a Dios que bendiga y proteja a estos esposos a quienes ha enriquecido con el sacramento del matrimonio.

Todos oran en silencio durante un breve espacio de tiempo. Luego, el celebrante y los padres extienden las manos. El celebrante prosigue:
(Tercera forma)

Padre santo, autor de todo el universo, que creaste a tu imagen al hombre y a la mujer y colmaste de bendiciones su unión conyugal, te pedimos por esta esposa que hoy se une a su marido por el sacramento del matrimonio.

Desciende, Señor, sobre ellos la abundancia de tu bendición (para que al gozo de su vida matrimonial añadan el encanto de los hijos y enriquezcan con ellos a tu Iglesia).

Que te alaben, Señor, en sus alegrías; que te busquen en sus tristezas; que en sus trabajos encuentren el gozo de tu ayuda y, en la necesidad, sientan cercano tu consuelo; que te invoquen en las reuniones sagradas; que den testimonio de ti entre los hombres y, después de una ancianidad feliz, lleguen al Reino de los Cielos acompañados de quienes hoy comparten su alegría. Por Cristo nuestro Señor. Amen.

De aquí en adelante, la Misa prosigue como de costumbre salvo que, después de la comunión, la esposa y el esposo, acompañados por el chambelán y la dama de honor, van al altar de la Virgen para rezar juntos; la esposa deja un ramo y el esposo quema un poco de incienso.

Rito de Despedida

NUPTIAL BLESSING

After the Lord's Prayer, the prayer "Deliver us" is omitted, and the parents of the bride and groom are invited to stand beside the presider.

Turned toward the couple, with hands joined, the presider invites the assembly to prayer, saying:

Brothers and sisters, let us ask God to bless and protect these newlyweds, who have been enriched by the sacrament of matrimony.

All pray silently for short while. Then the presider and the parents of the bride and groom extend their hands and the presider continues:

(Third form)

Holy Father, creator of the universe, maker of man and woman in your likeness, source of blessing for married life, we humbly pray to you for this woman who today is united with her husband in this sacrament of marriage.

May your fullest blessing come upon her and her husband so that they may together rejoice in your gift of married love (and enrich your church with their children).

Lord, may they both praise you when they are happy and turn to you in their sorrows. May they be glad that you help them in their work and know that you are with them in their need. May they pray to you in the community of the church and be your witnesses in the world. May they reach old age in the company of their friends and come at last to the kingdom of heaven. We ask this through Christ our Lord. Amen.

From this point on, the Mass continues as usual. After communion, however, the bride and groom, accompanied by the best man and maid of honor, go to the shrine of the Blessed Virgin to pray together. The bride leaves a bouquet, and the groom burns a small amount of incense. They then return to their places for the final blessing.

DISMISSAL RITE

꙳

Questions for Reflection

1. Aside from el pedir la mano, *are you aware of other Hispanic betrothal customs?*

2. What are the particular Hispanic marriage customs of this parish community? What are their origins?

3. What religious values are demonstrated in the exchange of rings, arras, libro y rosario *and the* ramo de la Virgen?

4. Is there a place in the parish liturgy for popular religious practices such as the blessing given by parents, grandparents and the elderly?

Rites Associated with Sickness and Death

Unción, Funeral, Velorio, Novenario y Levantacruz

utumn days are days of transition. In the Midwest they can be remarkably warm, sunny and bright. Yet there is a sudden chill in the breeze that sends a shudder up the spine, a reminder that winter is not far off. Fall days are for being outside as often as possible before winter's cold mandates self-enclosure.

This autumn Friday afternoon found Jon and Manuel home from work relaxing on the three-stair stoop of Manuel's apartment building. They were enjoying the end of the work week while sipping a cold drink. Sitting opposite one another, their conversation kept them oblivious to the noise of the kids on the street playing hide and seek, to the music of the radios perched on open window sills, to the raucous sounds of teenagers passing by and to the screech of a car's sudden stop.

Jon made no immediate connection with the popping noises he heard and the sudden change in Manuel's eyes. As if caught in slow motion, Manuel's drink slipped from his hand, bouncing and spilling on the stairs. Slowly leaning forward, he slumped onto Jon's shoulders. Within seconds, the terrible reality sank in as screams and speeding cars made Jon realize that Manuel had been shot. The next moments were a blur of color and emotion with the sudden onslaught of strangers trying to help, the appearance of Carmen from upstairs, the red ambulance lights and now the hospital calm while sitting in the emergency room's waiting area.

As Manuel's close friend and *compadre,* Jon was trying to bring order to the chaos in which he found himself. He was relieved when Father Kevin arrived. The priest's presence was an immediate reassurance to Carmen's and Manuel's families. They all sat in silence between bewildered questions and the status reports on the condition of the patient. Though numerous shots had been fired, only two had struck and done their deadly work. One had hit Manuel below his heart while the other traced a trail through his kidney. It was the doctor's suggestion that Father Kevin "do what he needed to do" before Manuel went to surgery.

The treatment room was barely able to contain both the feelings and family that filled it. While going about their duties, the hospital staff knew that this healing rite was as important as their own work. Father Kevin's words, though brief, focused this moment with memorized passages from scripture. His careful anointing of Manuel's head and hands was a sign of the tenderness of God's care, which brought peace to those present. Kevin understood that he could not prolong this moment but that everyone there also needed to express themselves. He did this by inviting them to come up and bless Manuel by tracing a cross on his forehead as they left. Carmen, Jon and Kevin were the last to bless Manuel and place him in God's hands before the doctors and nurses

moved him to surgery. Filled with hope, they retraced their steps to the waiting room.

Manuel never regained consciousness. In the fifty-fourth year of his life, he died in the intensive care unit with those he loved surrounding him. Jon called Kevin conveying Carmen's wish that they all meet in order to prepare the details of Manuel's funeral. After arranging the time and place, Kevin sat quietly and sadly, knowing that he would put up no argument as to what now needed to be done. His favorite adversary had walked him through these moments on too many other occasions, only now they would be felt and lived more intensely.

Kevin arrived at Carmen's house at the appointed hour. The five-room apartment was filled with the hushed noise of family and friends, the sweet aromatic fragrances of food cooking, the sporadic efforts of children trying to be quiet. He made his way through the crowd and found Carmen, like the sorrowful mother, surrounded by women — those of her family and Manuel's. She rose to greet Kevin with tearful but strong eyes. The two immediately began to talk about what needed to be done.

The wake service would consist of the rosary and scripture service with which everyone was familiar. It would be led by Kevin, Ana and Jon. Volunteers from the parish would sing. At the funeral Mass, all the family members would enter with white roses which would be placed on Manuel's casket. A family candle would be lit from the paschal candle and then placed on the altar. The readings would be read by their various *compadres* with their whole families accompanying them at the ambo. The final commendation would include a *pésame* by Jon and a word of gratitude by Jesús. The interment would take place at the graveside so that everyone might have a chance to offer a final blessing to Manuel with a handful of dirt and flowers.

After the funeral, rites for Manuel would continue with the traditional *novenario por los difuntos* — novena for the dead. Various *compadres* would lead the *novenario* that Kevin and Manuel had designed for the parish. As the name implies, it would be offered for nine consecutive evenings. On the last night of the novena, Kevin would celebrate Mass at their home. During the Mass, he would bless the cross already marked with the important dates of Manuel's life. The cross and his picture would then be enshrined in the *altarcito* of his home. Everything was so familiar to them both, yet it seemed strange, as if they were going through this for the first time. The services would help them all get through these days and the days that would follow. Kevin held Carmen for a moment before retreating to the back porch where the men had gathered. Immediately, Carmen was again comforted by the women who surrounded her.

Pastoral Notes

The preceding vignette narrates an all too common tragedy. It also allows us a glimpse at the way in which Hispanic/Latino families come to grips with diminishment and death. Hispanics, like others, do not generally experience crucial life events such as birth, coming of age, sickness and death as things that happen just to the individuals directly involved. These moments are lived out intensely in the context of the family — just as the joyful events such as baptism and first communion bring the family together, so the sickness or death of one member of the immediate or extended family affects all its members. If a pastoral approach is to be effective, it must go beyond a narrow focus on the one who is sick and include the members of the larger, extended family, both in ministry to the one who is sick as well as comfort to one another. This makes good pastoral sense in most situations, but is especially important in a Hispanic context. Let us take a quick look at the issues to which pastoral ministers need to be sensitive during these moments.

The experience of serious sickness and death is chronicled in a family's heart. This chronicle is regularly opened and read by its members. The domestic rituals and church liturgies that accompany these moments provide sources of spiritual as well as emotional strength that help all involved to bear the burden and to transcend this experience of human limitation. Adults, by example, initiate their children into these experiences. When death occurs, children learn that it is part of life. It sometimes comes as an uninvited guest, but consistent with the Hispanic value of hospitality, it is granted a place within the family. These rituals are rites of passage that rely much more on the way things are done than on the exact words said or the formulas used. The light of the paschal mystery makes these crises all the more heartfelt.

It is helpful to note that there are two different but related views among Hispanics on sickness and death, both of which need to be taken into account in ministering in this context. First, for many Latinos the illness of a family member is interpreted as a punishment from God. Something has gone wrong, and God is calling the family to conversion by inflicting this test on one of its members. God needs to be appeased through intensified prayer and sacrifices. Intercessory prayer of all kinds expresses this conversion. In this light, people's rituals are seen through the use of *promesas* (promises), *mandas* to make a pilgrimage, light candles, pray novenas, rosaries, offer Masses and other sacrificial activities in order to bring about healing from a benevolent God.

The second view on human diminishment is one of passive resignation — almost fatalism. If illness is seen as an instrument of divine justice, who can escape the hand of God? Expressions such as *es su destino* (it is his/her destiny) or *estaba escrito* (it was written) become the way many Latinos approach the serious illness and death of a loved one. Yet this worldview represents a double-edged sword, since there can be more than just a fatalistic acceptance of sickness and mortality. A common expression heard during these moments is *Resignarse a la voluntad de Dios.* A literal but incomplete translation renders the phrase "to resign oneself to the will of God," implying a passivity that does not exist in the Spanish. The sense of *resignarse* is to place oneself into God's hands, to abandon oneself to God's will. The last cry of Jesus on the cross, "Father, into your hands I commend my spirit," more accurately represents the meaning of *resignarse:* a conscious surrender to God's plan.

Sickness through disease, accident or random act of violence is attended to in the Hispanic community not through words but through presence. Pastoral presence may mean just sitting with the family. Spending time with the extended family becomes an important part of the "ritual." The shadow of the Tridentine notion of sacramental anointing as "extreme unction" still clouds the experience of the sacrament of the sick. Thankfully, this is changing as more and more parishes provide regular communal anointings at Mass. Paradoxically, even though catechesis and preaching may stress that those who receive sacramental anointing are the elderly, the gravely ill or those suffering from serious chronic illness, sickness in the Hispanic perspective is more encompassing. Its presence is often interpreted as weakness stemming not only from physical diminishment but also from emotional or spiritual troubles.

The practice of anointing fits well into the Hispanic way of healing for two reasons, one very traditional and the other more contemporary. First, healing is often associated with faith healers. Within the Mexican and Mexican American communities they are known as *curanderos(as).* In Caribbean countries they are called *santeros* or *espiritistas* and are similar but not the same as *curanderos.* This reflects the influence of African religions in these countries. It is beyond the scope of these pastoral notes to say more than that the healings of *curanderos* or *santeros* occupy a place in the Hispanic spiritual world. The pastoral minister needs to have an open mind and heart when dealing with these questions of healing. Secondly, *la renovación carismática* (charismatic renewal) is an important movement within the Hispanic community. *Círculos de oración* regularly hold healing services as a part of their gatherings. A confusion with the sacrament of anointing of the sick may arise, since conferring a blessing using oil often takes place in these services. Faith healing and charismatic anointing services nuance the Hispanic understanding of this sacrament.

Velorio (Wake)

Death is seen as part of life. Though sad, it is the occasion for another kind of *fiesta* in which domestic rituals of prayer, food, drink and storytelling help celebrate the life of the deceased and console the living. November 2, officially called *Fiesta de Todos los Fieles Difuntos,* is popularly known as *Día de los Muertos,* an annual family renewal linking the present generation with the ancestors. Remembering a person who has died is more than a nostalgic journey into the past. Remembering carries an anamnetic quality with it that renders the dear departed present to those who are left behind and who continue to provide for the well-being of those whom they love. On this day, visits to the cemetery, elaborate home altars to the dead, special breads, the eucharist in the church and special prayers all bring home the memory of those who have fallen asleep in the Lord. Candied skulls *(calaveras)* and papier maché dancing skeletons make fun of death and "its sting" by embracing its inevitability. Remembering is also the focus of the anniversary Masses traditionally offered one month after death and then every year. These are crucial days in a family's faith and life.

In a certain sense the wake *(velorio)*, funeral and *novenario* (the prayer service celebrated every day for nine days after the funeral) initiate the dead into a new way of participating in the life of the family. These celebrations express Paul's conviction that "if we have died with Christ, we believe that we shall live with him" (Romans 6:5). It should be remembered that just as the use of the terms Hispanic and Latino are a generalization for a very diverse cultural community, funerary customs can be generalized but vary a great deal from ethnic group to ethnic group. It is therefore important for the pastoral minister to ask questions about just how much he or she is expected to participate or lead the rites surrounding the funeral. The "professional" parish ministers should not feel threatened or feel pushed out of the way if the family invites *rezanderos(as)* (persons who know the traditional prayers and rituals by heart) to lead rosaries at the wake or the *novenario*.

When death visits a Hispanic family, the extended family, neighbors and friends descend upon the home with food, drink and *el pésame* (condolences). One of the traditional ways of expressing the *pésame* is to say, *"Te acompaño en tus sentimientos,"* which literally means, "I accompany you in your feelings (of grief)." This accompaniment does not try to take away the pain of death. Rather, it attempts to walk with, share in, and bear the burden with the bereaved. In the wake or *velorio*, the traditional rites consist of a specially prayed rosary, a Marian litany and prayers. In Hispanic devotion, Mary is seen as a family member who knows what it means to lose a loved one to suffering and death. Her intercession is a source of consolation. New, scripturally-based wake services need to take this into account. Rosary and scripture are not mutually exclusive but offer an opportunity for getting at the heart of the Hispanic experience of death. In what follows we offer a possible format for such a service, principally in Spanish. Experience has taught us that these domestic rituals are most effectively celebrated in the language of the heart.

A Sample Wake Service

The rosary is often requested at the wake service. At times there are people within the community who are called upon to lead the rosary. This indicates that it is a prayer of the community in which the majority of the people take part.

If the priest or deacon should decide to lead the rosary, he may begin with an Our Father, announce the first mystery and lead the ten Hail Marys, ending with the Glory Be. The rosary may be prayed one decade after another, or it may be embellished with songs, scripture, a homily and special prayers for the dead. The following is a suggested format.

MISTERIOS DEL ROSARIO

Misterios Gozosos

1. La Encarnación del Hijo de Dios
2. La Visita de Nuestra Señora a suprima Isabel
3. El Nacimiento del Hijo de Dios
4. La Purificación de Nuestra Señora
5. El Niño perdido en el Templo

Misterios Dolorosos

1. La Oración del Huerto
2. Los azotes que Jesús recibió atado a la columna
3. La Coronación de Espinas
4. Jesús con la Cruz a cuestas
5. La Crucifixión y Muerte de Jesús

Misterios Gloriosos

1. La Gloriosa Resurrección
2. La Ascensión
3. La Venida del Espíritu Santo
4. La Asunción de Nuestra Señora
5. La Coronación de Nuestra Señora

Líder, primer misterio:
Padre Nuestro, que estás en el cielo, santificado sea tu nombre, venga tu reino, hágase tu voluntad en la tierra como en el cielo;
Todos:
danos hoy nuestro pan de cada día; perdona nuestras ofensas, como también nosotros perdonamos a los que nos ofenden; no nos dejes caer en tentación, y líbranos del mal. Amén.

(10 Ave Marías)

Líder: Dios te salve, María, llena eres de gracia, el Señor es contigo, bendita tú eres entre todas las mujeres, y bendito es el fruto de tu vientre, Jesús.
Todos: Santa María, Madre de Dios, ruega por nosotros pecadores, ahora y en la hora de nuestra muerte. Amén.

Gloria
Líder: Gloria al Padre y al Hijo y al Espíritu Santo.
Todos: Como era en el principio, ahora y siempre, y por los siglos de los siglos. Amén.

Canto
Dios mío, Dios mío, acércate a mí,
Paloma sedienta que vuela hacia ti.
Quién dará a mi pecho como el alhelí rocío
que apague la sed que hay en mí.
Beber de tu cáliz al mundo es morir,
y morir al mundo es dulce vivir.

Segundo misterio:
Evangelio: Lucas 23:39 – 43
Líder: Lectura del santo Evangelio según San Lucas

Uno de los malhechores colgados le insultaba: "¿No eres tú el Cristo? Pues, ¡sálvate a ti y a nosotros!" Pero el otro le reprendió, diciendo: "¿Es que no temes a Dios, tú que sufres la misma

condena? Y nosotros con razón, porque nos lo hemos merecido con nuestros hechos; en cambio, éste nada malo ha hecho". Y decía: "Jesús, acuérdate de mí cuando vayas a tu reino". Jesús dijo: "Yo te aseguro: Hoy estarás conmigo en el Paraíso".
Palabra de Dios.

Tercer misterio:

Salmo 122

Lector: Vamos a la casa del Señor.

T: Vamos a la casa del Señor.

Lector: Qué alegría cuando me dijeron:
"Vamos a la casa del Señor".
Ya están pisando nuestros pies
tus umbrales, Jerusalén.

T: Vamos a la casa del Señor.

Lector: Jerusalén está fundada
como ciudad bien compacta.
Allá suben las tribus,
las tribus del Señor,
según la costumbre de Israel
a celebrar el nombre del Señor.

T: Vamos a la casa del Señor.

Lector: En ella están los tribunales de justicia,
en el palacio de David.
Desead la paz a Jerusalén:
"Vivan seguros los que te aman,
haya paz dentro de tus muros,
seguridad en tus palacios".

T: Vamos a la casa del Señor.

Lector: Por mis hermanos y compañeros voy a decir:
"La paz contigo". Por la casa del Señor,
nuestro Dios, te deseo todo bien.

T: Vamos a la casa del Señor.

Cuarto misterio:

H o m i l í a

Mis queridos hermanos y hermanas en Cristo: Nos hemos
reunido en oración esta noche como comunidad cristiana. La
muerte nos ha traído aquí y nos hace ver nuestros límites
como seres humanos. Por eso, nos consolamos los unos a los
otros con nuestra presencia humana, y así vemos la presencia
divina entre nosotros.

Jesucristo, nuestro Señor, quien pasó de la muerte a
la gloria, nos acompaña y nos consuela. Por Cristo sabemos
que la muerte es una transformación de nuestros cuerpos
mortales y es un vivir en Dios por siempre. Así, como familia
de Dios que somos, seguimos orando, por la intercesión de
la Virgen María, al beneficio de nuestro(a) hermano(a) y para
el beneficio de la Iglesia que formamos en Cristo nuestro Señor.

(Para concluir)

Quinto misterio:

Líder: Dios te salve, Reina y Madre de misericordia, vida, dulzura y esperanza nuestra; Dios te salve. A ti clamamos los
desterrados hijos de Eva; a ti suspiramos, gimiendo y llorando,
en este valle de lágrimas. Ea, pues, Señora, Abogada nuestra,
vuelve a nosotros esos tus ojos misericordiosos; y después
de este destierro, muéstranos a Jesús, fruto bendito de tu vientre.
¡Oh clementísima, oh piadosa, oh dulce Virgen María!

Oración

Líder: Oremos

Señor Dios, te ofrecemos nuestras oraciones en unión con
la Santísima Virgen María. La semilla muere en la tierra para
dar vida; te pedimos que des la vida eterna a nuestro(a) her-
mano(a), N. Consuélanos en esta muerte mientras celebramos

la resurrección de tu Hijo Jesucristo, que vive contigo y en
la unidad del Espíritu Santo por los siglos de los siglos. Amén.

The Funeral

The funeral Mass affords the opportunity to bring families and their
rituals into the structure of the liturgy. In addition to the rich
symbolism of the "standard rite" — sprinkling with water as a reminder
of baptism, the pall evoking the white baptismal garment and being
clothed in Christ, and the presence of the paschal candle — religious
objects that were dear to the deceased reverently placed on the coffin
all serve to focus the memories of those present on the Christian
life of the deceased.

Interment at Catholic cemeteries usually involves a chapel service
where family and friends say their final goodbyes. Though they are
well-intentioned, these places offer a rather sanitized image of death,
and they distance the mourners from the reality of the grave. For
many Hispanics the connection with the earth is most important and
evocative of how death is traditionally acknowledged on Ash Wednesday:
"Remember you are dust and to dust you shall return." Although a
graveside service is more expensive, for many Hispanic families it is the
right way to bury the dead. Sprinkling flower petals and dirt onto the
coffin expresses our personal connection and acceptance of this moment.
To return to the earth means to return to the place of our birth. This
can be taken both metaphorically as well as literally when the deceased
is returned to his/her native country.

Novenario

The *novenario*, the nine-day series of prayers, begins the day of interment. Usually a *rezandero/a* is appointed to lead the family in the
traditional rosary and litany for the dead. While respecting this practice,

we present below the first night of the *novenario*, based on the cathedral office for vespers. Just as the nine days mark a journey of accompaniment for family and friends, so does the new *novenario* mark each of these days in the light of a larger liturgical tradition.

> *Novenario: Primera noche*
> *Canto: Oh María, Madre Mía*
> María, Madre Mía
> Oh Consuelo del mortal
> Amparadme y guiadme
> A la patria celestial.
> Salve, Júbilo del cielo,
> Del excelso dulce imán:
> Salve, hechizo de este suelo
> Triunfador de Satán.
> Oh María, Madre Mía. . . .
> Del eterno las riquezas
> Por ti logro disfrutar
> Y contigo sus finezas
> Para siempre publicar.
> Oh María, Madre Mía. . . .
> *Líder:* Oh Dios, ven en nuestra ayuda.
> *Todos:* Señor, date prisa a socorrernos.
>
> *Líder:* Ave María Purísima,
> *Todos:* Sin pecado concebida.
> *Rosario: El de siempre hasta las glorias; entonces termina con la antífona tradicional (the rosary is prayed in the usual manner ending with the traditional antiphon).*
> *Líder:* Dále, Señor, el descanso eterno,
> *Todos:* Y brille para él (ella) la luz perpetua.
>
> *Al final y después de terminar los cinco misterios:*
> *Líder:* Padre Nuestro. . . .

Líder: Dios te salve, María, servidora fiel en la peregrinación terrenal, te encomiendo mi fe para que la ilumines, llena eres de gracia. . . .

Todos: Santa María. . . .

Líder: Dios te salve, María, testigo digna en seguir la voluntad de Dios, te encomiendo mi esperanza para que la alientes, llena eres de gracia. . . .

Todos: Santa María. . . .

Líder: Dios te salve, María, modelo de servicio y de entrega para el bien de los otros, te encomiendo mi amor cristiano para que lo aumentes, llena eres de gracia. . . .

Todos: Santa María. . . .

Letanía tradicional (opción)

Señor, ten piedad.

 R: Señor, ten piedad.

Cristo, ten piedad.

 R: Cristo, ten piedad.

Señor, ten piedad.

 R: Señor, ten piedad.

Cristo, óyenos.

 R: Cristo, óyenos.

Crito, escúchanos.

 R: Cristo, escúchanos.

Dios Padre celestial.

 R: Ten misericordia de nosotros.

Dios, Hijo Redentor del mundo.

 R: Ten misericordia de nosotros.

Dios Espíritu Santo.

 R: Ten misericordia de nosotros.

Santa María,

 R: Ruega por nosotros.

Santa Madre de Dios . . .

Santa Virgen de las vírgenes,
Madre de Cristo,
Madre de la Iglesia,
Madre de la divina gracia,
Madre purísima,
Madre castísima,
Madre y Virgen,
Madre inmaculada,
Madre amable,
Madre admirable,
Madre del Buen Consejo,
Madre del Creador,
Madre del Salvador,
Virgen prudentísima,
Virgen digna de veneración,
Virgen digna de alabanza,
Virgen poderosa,
Virgen acogedora,
Virgen fiel,
Ideal de santidad,
Trono de sabiduría,
Causa de nuestra alegría,
Templo del Espíritu Santo,
Obra maestra de la Gracia,
Modelo de entrega a Dios,
Rosa escogida,
Fuerte como torre de David,
Hermosa como torre de marfil,
Casa de oro,
Arca de la Nueva Alianza,
Puerta del cielo,

Estrella de la mañana,

Salud de los enfermos,

Refugio de los pecadores,

Consoladora de los afligidos,

Auxilio de los cristianos,

Reina de los Angeles,

Reina de los Patriarcas,

Reina de los Profetas,

Reina de los Apóstoles,

Reina de los Mártires,

Reina de los Confesores de la fe,

Reina de las Vírgenes,

Reina de todos los Santos,

Reina concebida sin pecado original,

Reina llevada al cielo,

Reina del santo Rosario,

Reina de la Paz.

Cordero de Dios, que quitas el pecado del mundo,

   R: Perdónanos, Señor.

Cordero de Dios, que quitas el pecado del mundo,

   R: Escúchanos, Señor.

Cordero de Dios, que quitas el pecado del mundo,

   R: Ten misericordia de nosotros.

Ruega por nosotros, Santa Madre de Dios.

   R: Para que seamos dignos de alcanzar las promesas

de Cristo.

Canto (opción)

   Resucitó, Resucitó, Resucitó Aleluya.

   La muerte, ¿Dónde está la muerte,

   dónde está mi muerte,

   dónde su victoria?

   Gracias sean dadas al Padre,

que nos pasó a su Reino
donde se vive de amor.
Resucitó, Resucitó, Resucitó, Aleluya.

Monición
Líder/Lector: Con el rezo del salmo expresamos un intenso acto
de confianza, y la esperanza de llegar al "país de la vida"
aumenta en nuestra comunidad.

Salmo 26:1 – 4, 13 – 14
Lector: El Señor es mi luz y mi salvación.
R: El Señor es mi luz y mi salvación.

Lector: El Señor es mi luz y mi salvación,
   ¿A quién temeré?
   El Señor es la defensa de mi vida,
   ¿Quién me hará temblar?
R: El Señor es mi luz y mi salvación.

Lector: Una cosa pido al Señor,
   eso buscaré:
   habitar en la casa del Señor
   por los días de mi vida;
   gozar de la dulzura del Señor
   contemplando su templo.
R: El Señor es mi luz y mi salvación.

Lector: Espero gozar de la dicha del Señor
   en el país de la vida.
   Espera en el Señor, sé valiente,
   ten ánimo, espera en el Señor.
R: El Señor es mi luz y mi salvación.

Oración

Lector: Oremos. . . .

Padre, al salir de esta tierra logramos la dicha prometida a
todos los que han sido fieles a tu ley. Concede a tu siervo(a)
un lugar en tu casa, y a nosotros la fuerza para seguir adelante
en nuestra peregrinación terrenal. Pedimos esto en el nombre
de nuestro Señor Jesucristo, que vive y reina contigo por
los siglos de los siglos.

Todos: Amén.

Abrazo

Lector: Démonos el saludo de la paz.

Bendición

Lector: El Señor nos bendiga, nos guarde de todo mal y nos
lleve a la vida eterna.

Todos: Amén.

(Persignándose)

Lector: Que la bendición de Dios, Padre, Hijo y Espíritu Santo
descienda sobre nosotros ahora y siempre.

Todos: Amén.

Levantacruz

The final day of the *novenario* closes with the rosary and prayers.
It can also conclude with a Mass, which would usher in a practice
common in some parts of Latin America wherein the dead are
commemorated monthly as well as annually. What is presented here
is a family's particular custom of "enthroning" the deceased in their
homes by raising a cross marked with the dates of his/her life
either during a home Mass or at the conclusion of the *novenario*.
These two celebrations continue the healing process as well
as keep the memory of the dead alive within a Hispanic family.

At the end of Mass or the *novenario* rosary, a good friend of the family or the presider presents the family with a red, cloth-covered cross which has been engraved with the dates of the life of the deceased. The rite continues with the singing or reverential reading of the following traditional hymn:

VED LA CRUZ DE SALVACION

Ved la cruz de salvación
donde Dios nos dio la vida;
precio de la redención
de la humanidad perdida
CRUZ DE CRISTO VENCEDOR
TE ADORAMOS, SALVANOS.
Arbol santo e inmortal,
son tus frutos redentores:
gracia, luz, perdón y paz
brindas a los pecadores.
Ara donde se inmoló
el cordero inmaculado:
Cristo en ti nos redimió
de la muerte y del pecado.
Nave firme en el luchar
con las olas de la vida;
faro en nuestro caminar
a la patria prometida.
Cruz de Cristo triunfador,
prenda de nuestra victoria;
Juez y discriminador
del infierno o de la Gloria.
Santo emblema del amor
fiel recuerdo del amada,
cruz que dice el pecador
la malicia del pecado.

Santa cruz de redención
arcoiris de alianza
signo eterno del perdón,
fuente viva de esperanza.

While a member of the family holds the cross, the presider (echoing the Good Friday veneration of the cross) uncovers its four parts while proclaiming the following prayers:

Unveiling the top of the cross:

Señor Jesús,
por los dolores que sufriste
en tu sagrada cabeza coronada de espinas,
te pedimos que perdones los pecados cometidos
por nuestro(a) hermano(a) con el pensamiento.
Padrenuestro . . .

Unveiling the right arm of the cross:

Señor Jesucristo,
por el dolor que sufriste
cuando un clavo traspasó tu mano derecha,
te pedimos que perdones los pecados
que nuestro(a) hermano(a)
haya cometido con su mano derecha.
Padrenuestro . . .

Unveiling the left arm of the cross:

Señor Jesucristo,
por el dolor que sufriste
cuando te clavaron la mano izquierda,
perdona los pecados que haya cometido
nuestro(a) hermano(a)
con su mano izquierda.
Padrenuestro . . .

Unveiling the bottom of the cross:
Señor Jesús,
por los dolores que sufriste
en todo tu cuerpo en el momento en que
    estabas crucificado,
perdona los pecados
que nuestro(a) hermano(a) haya cometido
con todo su cuerpo y su corazón.
Padre Nuestro, Ave María y
Dale Señor el descanso eterno . . .
R: Y brille para él (ella) la luz perpetua.
The prayer ends with a traditional hymn, such as "Victoria, tú reinarás."
The cross is then enthroned in the family's altarcito.

≈≈

Questions for Reflection

1. What are the stories, myths, jokes about sickness and death within the different cultural groups of your area and parish?

2. We are taught the meaning of sickness and suffering as we grow up. Can you as a pastoral minister or parishioner share the meaning of suffering in your life? What gospel patterns are reflected in your story?

3. What color is associated with death for the people of your community? What particular rituals, hymns, customs, prayers or rites help the family to bear their grief? Are any of these associated with the funeral liturgy?

4. Crosses come in many shapes, styles, colors and designs. Are there particular crosses associated with mourning — from traumatic grief to quiet acceptance to peace of heart?

5. How is death accepted as a sign of life in your heart, in the heart of your community?

Epilogue

The autumn breeze came through the bedroom window that morning like the soothing touch of a loved one. Manuel stood at the foot of the bed, half smiling, half smirking at the situation. As he looked upon Carmen sleeping gently in the breeze's embrace, she felt his loving presence cover her once again. Carmen stirred herself awake expecting to see him standing there once again. In not opening her eyes to the reality of the emptiness, she ached to hold him close to her. The baby's penetrating cry pierced the quiet, reminding her that she was not alone. Jesús and Anita had left their firstborn with Carmen for the night. Now he demanded attention.

In the kitchen Carmen held the baby bottle and baby while placing a call to Father Kevin. She hopes to catch him early in order to clarify the details for tonight's Saturday Mass. Jon and Ana had made all the necessary calls asking everyone not to be late. It was to be a special celebration. Tonight was the first-year anniversary of Manuel's death. Surprising everyone, as she was accustomed to doing, Carmen suggested that it would be an appropriate night to have the *presentación del niño* for Jesús's and Anita's baby. Father Kevin at first hesitated, but Carlos saw the inner logic. Jon felt Manuel's influence in this. Ana admired her *comadre's* good family sense. Carmen simply thought that Manuelito should know his namesake's love for his family, his religion and his traditions. Standing in the cool morning air of the open kitchen window, with the newborn child feeding tranquilly in her arms, Carmen knew it was the right thing to do.

Recursos/Resources

GENERAL

Bravo, Benjamín, ed., *Diccionario de Religiosidad Popular.* México, 1992.

Departmento de Liturgia de la Arquidiócesis de Lima. *Manual Litúrgico,* iv edición, "Aclamación de la Asamblea" (Lima: Ediciones Paulinas, 1992): 166 – 167

Escamilla, Roberto. "Worship in the Context of the Hispanic Culture," *Worship* 51 (1977): 290 – 293.

Favoretto, Bernardo. *Ritual para Laicos.* San Pablo: Caracas, Venezuela, 1993.

Figueroa-Deck, Allan. "Liturgy and Mexican American Culture," *Modern Liturgy* 3:7 (1976): 24 – 26.

Garcia Ibarra, Jesús. *Manual de Celebraciones Sacramentales,* "Monición de Entrada" (México, D.F.: Libreria Parroquial de Clarería, 1992): 254.

Hays, Edward. *Oraciones de la familia hispana para todas ocasiones.* Chicago: Claretian Publications, 1981.

Hays, K. and Pérez, A. "Worship in a Multicultural Community," *Liturgy* 80 (May/June, 1986): 13 –14.

Icaza, Rosa María. "Prayer, Worship and Liturgy in a U.S. Hispanic Key," in Allan Figueroa Deck, ed., *Frontiers of Hispanic Theology in the United States.* Maryknoll, New York: Orbis, 1992, 134 –153.

Icaza, Rosa María, "Espiritualidad — Mística — Liturgia," in Galerón, S., Icaza, R., Urrabazo, R., eds., *Visión Profética: Reflexiones Pastorales sobre el Plan Pastoral Para el Ministerio Hispano.* Kansas City: Sheed & Ward, 1992, 65–72 (Español); 239–247 (English).

Instituto de Liturgia Hispana, FDLC, "Guidelines for Multilingual Masses," *Liturgy 80* (February/March, 1987): 6–7.

Office of Research and Planning, Archdiocese of Newark. *Presencia Nueva: Knowledge for Service and Hope — A Study of Hispanics in the Archdiocese of Newark.* Newark: Office of Research and Planning, 1988.

Pequeño Ritual para Sacramentales, Sacramentos, Oraciones y Otros Ritos en algunas Circunstancias. Guadalajara, Jal. Secretaria del Arzobispado, 1985.

Pérez, Arturo. "The History of the Hispanic Liturgy since 1965," in J.P. Dolan and A.F. Deck, eds., *Hispanic Catholic Culture in the U.S.: Issues and Concerns.* Notre Dame, IN: University of Notre Dame Press, 1994, 360–408.

Ramirez, R. "Hispanic Approach to Sunday Worship," *Liturgy 70* (April, 1979): 3–5.

Ramirez, R. "Liturgy from the Mexican American Perspective." *Worship* 51 (1977): 350–366.

Ramirez, R. "Reflections on the Hispanization of the Liturgy." *Worship* 57 (1983): 26–34.

Ramirez, R. "The State of Hispanic Liturgy in the United States," *Liturgy 80* (August/September, 1989): 7–8.

Ritual Completo de los Sacramentos: textos litúrgicos oficiales aprobados para México. Compilados y anotados por Pedro I. Rovalo, sj, y equipo dela Comisíon Episcopal de Liturgia. México, D.F.: Obra Nacional de la Buena Prensa, 1976.

Ritual Conjunto: Celebración del Bautismo, Matrimonio, Eucaristía fuera de la Misa. Comisíon Episcopal de Liturgia, Chile. Santiago: Librería San Pablo, 1987.

Ritual del Matrimonio, sexta edición. Barcelona: Comisión Episcopal Española de Liturgia, 1971.

Ritual del Matrimonio, tercera edición. Bogotá: Conferencia Episcopal de Colombia, 1987.

Ritual de las Exequias. Conferencia Episcopal de Colombia. Bogotá: SPEC Departamento de Liturgia, 1983.

Socías, James. *Oraciones/Prayers.* Chicago: Midwest Theological Forum, 1996.

Sosa, Juan. "Liturgia Hispana en los EE. UU.," *Notitiae* 20 (1984): 688 – 696.

Sosa, Juan. "Let us Pray . . . En Español," *Liturgy* 3:2 (1983): 63 – 67.

Sosa, Juan. "Texto Unico: A Unified Liturgical text for Spanish Speaking Catholics," *Liturgy* 80 (May/June, 1989): 9 –10.

Mexican American Cultural Center. *Faith Expressions of Hispanics in the Southwest.* Revised edition. San Antonio: Mexican American Cultural Center, 1990.

Perales, Jorge, ed., *Oracional Bilingüe/ A Prayer Book for Spanish English Communities.* Collegeville: The Liturgical Press, 1994.

POPULAR RELIGION AND LITURGY

Espin, Orlando. "Religiosidad Popular: Un Aporte Para su Definición y Hermenéutica," *Estudios Sociales* 17 (Octubre/Diciembre, 1984): 41– 56.

Figueroa Deck, Allan. "Popular Religiousness, Popular Catholicism," *The Second Wave: Hispanic Ministry and the Evangelization of Cultures.* Mahwah, NJ: Paulist Press, 1989: 113 –119.

Flores, Ricardo. "Para el Niño Dios: Sociability and Commemorative Sentiment in Popular Religious Practice," in Anthony M. Stevens-Arroyo & Ana María Díaz-Stevens, eds., *An Enduring Flame:*

Studies on Latino Popular Religiosity, New York: PARAL, 1994, 171–190.

Francis, Mark. "Hispanic Popular Piety and Liturgical Reform," *Modern Liturgy* 18 (1991): 14–17.

Francis, Mark. "Popular Piety and Liturgical Reform in a Hispanic Context," in Pineda & Schreiter, eds., *Dialogue Rejoined: Theology and Ministry in the United States Hispanic Reality.* Collegeville: The Liturgical Press, 1995, 162–177.

Galilea, Segundo. *Religiosidad Popular y Pastoral Hispano-Americana.* New York: Centro Católico de Pastoral para Hispanos del Nordeste, 1981.

Herrera, Marina. "Popular Devotions and Liturgical Education," *Liturgy* 5:1 (1985): 33–37.

Herrera, Marina. "Religion and Culture on the Hispanic Community as a Context for Religious Education: Impact of Popular Religiosity on U.S. Hispanics," *The Living Light* 21:2 (1985): 136–146.

Maldonado, Luis. *Introducción a la Religiosidad Popular.* Madrid: Sal Terrae, 1985.

Matovina, Tim, "Liturgy, Popular Rites, and Popular Spirituality," *Worship* 63 (1989): 351–361.

Matovina, Tim. "Liturgy and Popular Expressions of Faith: A Look at the Works of Virgil Elizondo," *Worship* 65 (1991): 436–444.

Pérez, Arturo. "Blessings: Ritual Resources for the Hispanic Community," *Liturgy 80* (June–July, 1983): 11–12.

Pérez, Arturo. *Popular Catholicism: A Hispanic Perspective.* Pastoral Press, 1988.

Religiosidad Popular: Las Imágenes de Jesucristo y la Virgen María en América Latina. San Antonio: Instituto de Liturgia Hispana, 1990.

Sosa, Juan. "An Anglo-Hispanic Dilemma: Liturgical Piety or Popular Piety," *Liturgy* 24:6 (1979): 7–9.

Sosa, Juan. "Popular Piety: An Integral Element of the Conversion Process," *Christian Initiation Resources*. Volume 1. New York: Sadlier, 1980, 249–254.

Vidal, Jaime. "Towards an Understanding of Synthesis in Iberian and Hispanic American Popular Religiosity," in Anthony M. Stevens-Arroyo & Ana María Díaz-Stevens, eds., *An Enduring Flame: Studies on Latino Popular Religiosity*. New York: PARAL, 1994, 69–96.

BAUTISMO

Brophy, Matt. "Presentación del Niño," *Liturgy 80* (February/March, 1986): 6–7.

MACC Pastoral Team. *The New Rite of Baptism/Nuevo Rito del Bautismo in Spanish and English*. San Antonio: Mexican American Cultural Center, 1991.

Mexican American Cultural Center. "La entrega formula," *Bilingual Rite of Baptism* (San Antonio, 1975): 14.

McKenzie, Don. "Restoring the Sequence of the Sacraments of Initiation with Children," *FDLC Newsletter* 23:2 (April–May, 1996): 9–12.

Pérez, Arturo. "Baptism in the Hispanic Community," *Emmanuel* (1981): 77–86.

CONFIRMACIÓN

Balhoff, M. "Age for Confirmation: Canonical Evidence," *The Jurist* 45 (1985): 549–587.

Huels, J. "The Age of Confirmation: A Canonist's View," *Catechumenate* 9 (1987): 30–36.

Lopez Vallejo, Alfredo. "Reflexión Pastoral sobre la Confirmación", *Actualidad Litúrgica* (Marzo/Abril, 1991): 28–34.

Llopis, J. "La Edad Para la Confirmación. Estado Actual del Problema", *Phase* 12 (1972): 237–248.

Turner, Paul. *Confirmation: The Baby in Solomon's Court*. Mahwah, NJ: Paulist, 1993

Wilde, James (ed.) *When Should We Confirm?* Chicago: Liturgy Training Publications, 1989.

QUINCE AÑOS

Cavillo Paz, Mateo. *Juicio sobre Quinceañeras en la Iglesia: Problemática Pastoral, Esquemas de Celebración*. México, D.F.: Librería Parroquial de Clavería, 1990.

Erevia, Angela. *Religious Celebration for the Quinceañera*. San Antonio: MACC, 1980.

Erevia, Angela. *Quince Años: Celebrando una tradición/Celebrating a Tradition*. San Antonio: Missionary Catechists of Divine Providence, 1985.

Mayer, Robert. "A Quinceañera Mass," *Modern Liturgy* 3:7 (1976): 28–29.

MATRIMONIO

Aróztegui, Xavier. "Bendición de los Esposos en el Aniversario del Matrimonio," *Liturgia y Espiritualidad* XXVI (7/8, Julio/Agosto): 1995.

Instituto de Liturgia Hispana. *Ritos Matrimoniales Hispanos*. Unpublished Manuscript.

Matovina, Timothy. "Marriage Celebrations in Mexican American Communities," *Liturgical Ministry* 5 (Winter, 1996): 22–26.

UNCIÓN, EXEQUIAS, NOVENARIOS

Butera, Luis. *Novenario Biblico para Difuntos*. México, D.F.: Ediciones Servidores de la Palabra, 1981.

Camps, Joseph and Lligadas, Josep. *Orar por los Difuntos.* Barcelona: Centre de Pastoral Litúrgica, 1981.

Erevia, Angela. "Death and Funerals in the Mexican American Community," *Pace* 10 (1979).

Erevia, Angela. *En Las Manos del Señor: Novenario de Difuntos.* San Antonio: Misioneras Catequistas de la Divina Providencia, 1993.

Pérez, Arturo. "Novenario," *Liturgy 80* (October, 1985):8–9; (November–December 1985): 13–14.

Pérez, Arturo. *Novenario por los Difuntos.* Chicago: Liturgy Training Publications, 1987.

Sosa, Juan. "Illness and Healing in Hispanic Communities," *Liturgy* 2:2 (1982): 65–68.